Discovering the Boston Harbor Islands

Also by Christopher Klein:

The Die-Hard Sports Fan's Guide to Boston: A Spectators Handbook

Union Park Press
PO Box 81435
Wellesley, MA 02481-0005
www.unionparkpress.com

Printed in China
Second Edition

Library of Congress Control Number: 2007909250

ISBN: 978-1-934598-06-1

Book design & production by Elizabeth Willett

Cover photographs (top) Nicole L. Vecchiotti (bottom) Lisa Teso

Discovering the

BOSTON HARBOR ISLANDS

A Guide to the City's Hidden Shores

Christopher Klein

BOSTON

UNION
PARK
PRESS

ISLAND HOPPING

Harbor & Island Resources

Icon Key

ACCESS

 Ferry / Inter-island Ferry

Private Craft Only

 Access Discouraged / Restricted

Car / Parking

Marina / Moorings

SIGHTS

Lighthouse

Fort

Historic Structures & Ruins

Arts & Culture

Special Interest

ACTIVITIES

Camping

Hiking / Walking Trails

Life-guarded Beach

Fishing

Birding

Kayaking

SERVICES

Food

Toilets

Information / Ranger Staffed

 Currently, there is ferry service to eight of the thirty-four harbor islands. Spectacle and Georges are considered hub islands. Ferry service leaves from Long Wharf in Boston to Georges and Spectacle Islands, and from the Fore River Shipyard in Quincy to Georges Island.

An inter-island ferry route runs from Georges Island to Lovells, Grape, Bumpkin, and Peddocks Islands along with the Hingham Shipyard and Pemberton Point in Hull. Please ask the crew onboard the mainland ferry about connecting to another island, as routes may change.

Timetables are available online at www.harborislands.org, or call 617-223-8666. The season runs from May to mid-October.

Special ferry service is provided to Thompson Island and Little Brewster Island. See those chapters for additional information.

 Spectacle Island Marina and island moorings are managed by Constitution Marina: 617-241-9640. To call Spectacle Island Marina: 857-452-7221 or hail VHF 69. Moorings are available at Long, Gallops, Georges, Rainsford, and Peddocks Islands. Docks are for drop off only.

 A number of islands are open to visitation, but lack docks; boaters who would like to go ashore will often need a flat-bottom raft, dinghy, or kayak.

For information about public programming, check online at www.harborislands.org.

See Resources for more information about recreational opportunities on and around the harbor islands.

Foreword

Boston is a city rich in culture and steeped in history, and with so much happening in the city's neighborhoods, it is sometimes easy to forget our city's proud maritime tradition. Our picturesque harbor gave birth to our city and sustains it to this very day. And the best way to experience Boston's nautical heritage is to visit the Boston Harbor Islands, where the city's past, present, and future await you.

Thanks to the many dedicated people and partners who have realized their vision of a national park area, the Boston Harbor Islands have been transformed from ignored relics into places of learning, entertainment, and recreation. Their history is fascinating, their present-day reclamation remarkable, and the vision of the future is exhilarating.

The islands have been reborn following the cleanup of Boston Harbor and the establishment of the national park area. Visitation to the area has doubled since 1996. Three islands have been newly opened to the public—including the harbor's newest star, Spectacle Island.

Kayakers, boaters, and swimmers are thrilled by the improved water quality. Recreational fishing is thriving with the rebounding fish population. Tales of ghosts, shipwrecks, and pirates enchant children of all ages. Nature lovers can hike and camp, and history buffs can learn about the times gone by of these majestic islands that helped to shape both our city and our country.

Each year more city residents and visitors from around the world discover the beauty of the harbor islands that lie just minutes away from downtown Boston. And as the Big Dig ends and the creation of the Rose Kennedy Greenway blooms, the city's reconnected historic waterfront will increasingly serve as a wonderful launching point for Boston's offshore riches.

Discovering the Boston Harbor Islands is an open invitation to explore the Boston of yore and to experience Boston's resilience. Enjoy!

— *Mayor Thomas M. Menino*

Portrait of the Harbor   *An Introduction*

As the crowd boards the ferry at Boston's Long Wharf, a sense of anticipation mingles with the smells of salt water and suntan lotion filling the air. Young children tote their sand pails. Their parents carry coolers with picnic supplies. Intrepid campers haul their gear and tents. The women of the Red Hat Society scour the itinerary for their afternoon outing. It's a diverse crowd, to be sure, but they all have one thing in common: they're embarking on an island adventure.

Within moments, the ferry is underway, passing the burgeoning South Boston Waterfront and gliding underneath the bellies of jumbo jets landing at Logan International Airport. Seagoing vessels of all varieties crowd the harbor. The spire of the Old North Church, the tower of the Custom House, and the rest of the city skyline dissolve in the mist, and a cool sea breeze tempers the sultry summer heat.

In no time at all the passengers arrive at their destination: Spectacle Island. It's a completely different world from the one they just left. The canyon walls of Boston's skyscrapers have been replaced by open skies. The chaos of the city streets has been supplanted by the tranquility of island life.

What is it about islands that speak to the adventurer in each of us? Why do we experience such a thrill at being surrounded by water, cut off from the rest of the world? Isolated and remote, romantic and invigorating, islands offer the promise of solitude and exploration as well as an intimate communion with the natural world in one of its most extreme designs. Few landscapes possess the same drama, magic, or mystery, and as the waves crash along the shoreline, life and its innumerable routines are somehow put into perspective. Perhaps the mystery lies in the voyage itself—whether you opt for the ferry, a kayak, or you are the captain of your own ship—the effort required to land on an island is integral to the overall experience. These miniature worlds, formed by a complex of geological forces, call on us to interact with our environment in ways that are increasingly less frequent.

Spectacle Island is just one of the jewels in the Boston Harbor Islands national park area, which includes thirty-four islands and coastal peninsulas in a twelve-mile radius from downtown Boston. And it is just one of thirty-four chances from which to see Boston in a new light. Long before Frederick Law Olmsted conceived of his Emerald Necklace of parkland ringing Boston, the Boston Harbor Islands formed a "Sapphire Necklace" draped around Boston Neck—the narrow peninsula on which Boston was originally built. No other major city in the United States is blessed with such an island-studded harbor. Yet, despite their proximity and the wide array of recreational opportunities, the Boston Harbor Islands are relatively unknown to millions who live within their easy reach. This is a shame, as the harbor islands offer a rare opportunity to visit unspoiled landscapes and wildlife features within the confines of an urban center. This urban oasis is an area of breathtaking beauty and spectacular vistas. Filled with colorful tales of hermits, ghosts, pirates, shipwrecks, and buried treasure, the ruins of forts and summer estates fascinate explorers of all ages. Like the ebbing and flowing tide, the city's history laps up on their shores, and the harbor islands are a prism through which we can view the history of Boston and, to a large extent, America.

It's not too grand a statement to say that Boston would not be the city it is today without its harbor islands. In fact, the islands built John Winthrop's nascent "city upon a hill." Timber from the mature forests that grew on the islands was used to construct homes and wharves. The slate quarried from their shores paved the city streets. Once denuded, livestock that grazed and crops that grew on the harbor islands fed the growing colony. What's more, the islands afforded Boston protection from nature's fury and enemy attack, creating one of the safest and most commodious harbors in the world, which in turn allowed Boston to become a thriving maritime power.

Indeed, nature proved to be a fine engineer when she designed Boston Harbor and sculpted its island cluster. The massive glaciers that engulfed Boston during the Ice Age more than 15,000 years ago left behind smooth mounds of sand, gravel, and rock called "drumlins"—in profile, they've been described as upside-down teaspoons. As the ice sheets melted, the water level rose, and the drumlins were surrounded by Boston Harbor, formed between the two outstretched arms of Winthrop and Hull that seem to clutch the islands in their warm embrace. (Bunker Hill and Beacon Hill are both drumlins as well.) Afloat within the vast estuary ecosystem formed by the salty Massachusetts Bay and the freshwater of the Charles, Mystic, and Neponset rivers, the Boston Harbor Islands are a geological rarity, forming the only drumlin "swarm" in the United States that intersects a coastline.

While the harbor islands have created natural breakwaters that bear the brunt of ferocious gales and the open sea, they have also provided easily defensible locations to protect Boston from enemy attack. From the establishment of a fort on Castle Island in 1634 until just after World War II, the Boston Harbor Islands were home to active military fortifications that deterred potential naval incursions, trained soldiers, and housed prisoners of war. In their darkest moment, the islands were used during King Philip's War in 1675 and 1676 to intern Native Americans.

For centuries, the Boston Harbor Islands have served as a gateway to Boston and America. For nearly three hundred years, the towering beacon of Boston Light on Little Brewster Island, the oldest light station in America, has been a welcome sight for thousands of tempest-tossed mariners arriving from around the world. Today, of course, most visitors to Boston arrive by air, but the islands outside the cabin windows still greet this new generation of travelers who touch down along the harbor shores at Logan Airport.

Boston Harbor, 1835. John S. Blunt. Photograph © Museum of Fine Arts, Boston.

Beginning in the 1840s, for the tens of thousands of immigrants starting a new life in a new land, the first piece of American soil on which these "huddled masses" stepped was often at the quarantine and immigration stations on the islands. In fact, so many immigrants passed through the Boston Harbor Islands that they were considered as an alternative site for the Statue of Liberty when New York City was having trouble raising money to build its pedestal in the early 1880s.

The rise in immigration nearly doubled the population of Boston between 1840 and 1860, and those seeking relief from the congested city sought out recreational activities in the harbor and on its islands. Island inns and resorts popped up during the nineteenth century. Summer colonies took root. And steamships crisscrossed the harbor bringing day trippers to and from island destinations. While most Bostonians took to the harbor to enjoy its cool, salubrious breezes, others sought out activities that were frowned upon by puritanical Boston. These remote, offshore locations provided the perfect venues for unsanctioned boxing matches, gambling, and opium parties.

Boston also turned to its harbor islands as a place to exile its sick and downtrodden and house its social institutions. The islands provided faraway places to sequester undesirable people and material that Bostonians didn't want in the city proper. In this regard, the history of the islands is very much the history of Boston's reform impulse. Reformatories, asylums, poorhouses, hospitals, and prisons were situated on many of the harbor islands. Likewise, as many as four islands were the home to quarantine stations, which protected the city from outbreaks of smallpox and other deadly, contagious diseases. Many victims of those diseases died on the islands, and today these forgotten cemeteries are as common as the ruins of old military installations.

Of course, as Bostonians know all too well, long before the colonists dumped their tea into the harbor, they were draining their sewage into it. The city also sent its garbage to the islands, and the Spectacle Island landfill is perhaps the most notorious example of the disregard Bostonians had for their islands and waterways. Centuries of this environmental degradation took their toll on the health of the harbor and its aquatic life, and by 1987, the water quality in Boston Harbor was so poor that the federal government identified it as the dirtiest in America. The banner headline across the top of the *Boston Herald* on April 28, 1987, said it all: "Harbor of Shame."

Though it's hard to fathom given the level of pollution, the islands were the last open frontier available for the continuing sprawl of Boston and under the threat of development throughout the 1960s and 1970s. The most sweeping proposal called for the construction of a high-rise apartment community—connected to downtown by subways, ferries, and bridges—that could house as many as 150,000 people. There were also proposals, building on Boston's long tradition of land-making, to fill in the harbor around some of the islands to build a new airport and a world's fair site. Islands—such as Apple, Bird, and Governor's—were indeed lost to this practice, and now remain buried somewhere beneath Logan Airport.

Luckily, the Boston Harbor Islands had their champions who fought to prevent development, clean up the harbor, and preserve their exquisite natural beauty. One of the most significant was the late Edward Rowe Snow, the master storyteller and historian who wrote over a hundred books on New England maritime history, many of which included stories about Boston Harbor and its islands. Through his writings and radio programs, Snow brought the lively history and legends surrounding the islands to the attention of a new generation of Bostonians. No one who followed

Snow on his tour through the dark corridors of Fort Warren will forget his tale of the Lady in Black. Snow's legions of fans and friends continue to hold a birthday party for him on Georges Island each August, and the Hull Lifesaving Museum sponsors its annual Snow Row each March on a course from Hull around the harbor islands.

Taking up Snow's mantle, advocates of the harbor and the islands successfully pressed in federal court during the 1980s for the $4.5 billion cleanup of Boston Harbor, the centerpiece of which was the new wastewater treatment plant on Deer Island that opened in 2001. Ruling that "the law secures to the people the right to a clean harbor," Federal District Court Judge A. David Mazzone served as a mighty force overseeing the cleanup project for nearly two decades. The project has transformed the harbor from one of the dirtiest to one of the cleanest, and it has led to a rebirth of the islands. Likewise, another major Boston construction project, the Big Dig, has transformed Spectacle Island from a garbage dump to the national park area's newest jewel.

The cleanup of the harbor played a pivotal role in the creation of the Boston Harbor Islands National Recreation Area in 1996. (Native Americans objected to the term "recreation area" to describe the islands where their ancestors were incarcerated and died during King Philip's War, so the islands are now referred to as a "national park area.") The national park area is unique in that the National Park Service owns none of its 1,600 acres, and the islands are owned and maintained by a complex partnership of federal, state, city, and nonprofit agencies, which seeks to maintain the right balance between the islands' role as a source for recreation and a preserve for scenery, wildlife, and historic sites.

With the completion of the Big Dig and the blossoming of the Rose Kennedy Greenway, Boston is rediscovering its waterfront and its nautical heritage. Inside the new Boston Harbor Islands Pavilion on the Greenway, interactive exhibits and interpretive panels enlighten a new generation to the endless number of adventures that can be found just a short boat ride away. History buffs can explore lighthouses, ruins, and the military installations that have protected Boston from the time of its founding through the Second World War. Adventure seekers can scuba dive amid centuries-old shipwrecks. Boaters can venture to the outer islands, a breathtaking ocean wilderness that marks the edge of civilization. Anglers can fish for striped bass, bluefish, and flounder in the revitalized harbor waters. The wandering trails on many of the islands are perfect for day-hikes, and several islands are available for overnight camping. Summer weekends provide a wide variety of cultural and educational programs—from old-time baseball games, jazz concerts, and art installations, to children's programs, citizen science activities, and ranger-led tours.

Nature lovers will be enthralled by the islands' diverse flora and fauna that thrive in a range of habitats from tidal salt marshes to rocky shores to woodlands. In many regards, the Boston Harbor Islands are New England's backyard Galapagos. With the loss of biodiversity on the planet at an all-time high, the harbor islands provide a natural laboratory for scientists and the public to explore nature's evolution and how multiple, diverse human impacts affect natural systems.

Botanists have identified more than five hundred plant species on the islands, many of them non-native due to changes in habitat caused by human deforestation or the introduction of invasive species. With more than 130 species of birds, including sixty-seven that have been found to breed on the islands, the Boston Harbor Islands are considered an Important Bird Area by organizations such as the Massachusetts Audubon Society. Small mammals, such as rabbits, raccoons, and foxes, have been found on the islands, and—thanks to the cleanup of the harbor—seals and porpoises have returned to the outer islands. Even tide pools along the shores are teeming with a micro-wilderness of aquatic life. These habitats serve as unique living class-rooms for Boston-area schoolchildren brought to the islands by nonprofit groups and summer camps.

In some respects, the undeveloped landscapes on many islands make it easy to imagine what this part of the world looked like when the first group of Puritans aboard

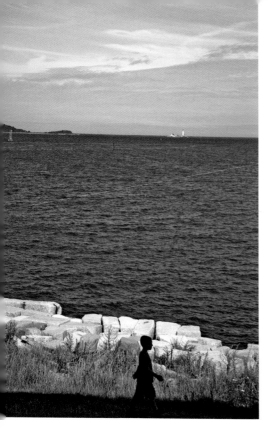

the *Arbella* passed by in 1630. Since then, these islands have had a front-row seat for some of the most seminal moments in the long sweep of American history: A tea party in 1773, which rippled through the harbor and grew into waves of freedom washing over America. The departure of the last British troops driven out by a band of colonists in 1776. The arrival of the first "coffin ships" carrying Irish famine victims in Black '47. The launch of Donald McKay's fleet clippers, such as the *Flying Cloud*, that would rule the seas in the 1850s. And the return of the celebrated 54th Massachusetts Volunteer Infantry Regiment from bloody Civil War battlefields.

But there is a quieter history of the islands, too, though no less important, and it speaks to the bond between Bostonians and the sea. As the last frontier in the Boston area, the islands tell us about the peopling of New England. From the Native Americans who seasonally camped on the islands, to the Portuguese fisherman who lived in shanties on their shores; from the Brahmins who built unapproachable estates high above the crashing waves, to the hermits who lived like castaways—the harbor islands are awash in the history of hearty New Englanders drawn to the ocean.

Each island of Boston Harbor has its own distinctive personality and its own story to tell, and this urban archipelago offers a unique chance to journey into nature and back into time—all within the shadows of the city skyline. So set sail. Pack your imagination and your love of adventure. There's an island out there, waiting for you.

1 **Scale to the top of Boston Light.** Take a guided tour of the oldest light station in the country and climb the seventy-six spiral steps and two short ladders to come face-to-face with the lighthouse's giant Fresnel lens.

2 **Take a dip.** Grab your bathing suit, towel, and suntan lotion and head to the sand and surf at Spectacle Island's new lifeguarded beach.

3 **Wander Fort Warren's dark passages.** Explore the spooky tunnels of this historic fort that once held Confederate prisoners during the Civil War.

4 **Pitch a tent.** Camp out on the islands and catch unforgettable sunrises and sunsets in the shadows of the city skyline. Spend the night on Grape Island for the most bucolic setting.

5 **Grab a paddle.** Beginning kayakers can spend the afternoon exploring the Hingham Harbor islands, while experienced kayakers can brave the outer harbor to visit the Brewsters.

6 **Scale Thompson Island's ropes and climbing walls.** Participate in one of Outward Bound's programs and challenge your limitations by conquering the ropes course and climbing towers.

7 **Pack a lunch.** There are fantastic spots to picnic on all the harbor islands, but the picnic areas on Bumpkin and Great Brewster Islands offer unparalleled vistas.

8 **Brush up on your fish tales.** Fish populations are rebounding along with the harbor's water quality. Striped bass, bluefish, flounder, and cod are among the fish that are biting.

9 **Follow your feathered friends.** Grab a pair of binoculars and try to spot some of the more than one hundred species of birds that frequent the Boston Harbor Islands.

10 **See Boston in a new light.** There's no better view of the city and harbor than from Spectacle Island's north drumlin. Private boaters can stay overnight at the marina—bring a chair for the Saturday night movie on the pier, or a blanket for the bonfire on the beach.

Island Hopping

PROVINCETOWN

CAPE COD BAY

CETOWN

SCITUATE

COHASSET

BUMKIN IS.

TO NANTASKET

HULL

HINGHAM

WEIR RIVER

PEDDOCK'S ISLAND

GEORGES ISLAND

LOUPS AND

RAINSFORD ISLAND

HOUGH'S NECK

LONG ISLAND

QUINCY BAY

MOON ISLAND

SQUANTUM

SPECTACLE ISLAND

THOMPSON'S ISLAND

DORCHESTER BAY

CASTLE ISLAND

PLEASURE BAY

MARINE PARK

SOUTH BOSTON

OLD HARBOR

SOUTH BAY

Inne

South Bost

Old H

Columbia Po

Dorchester

Map not intended for navigation.

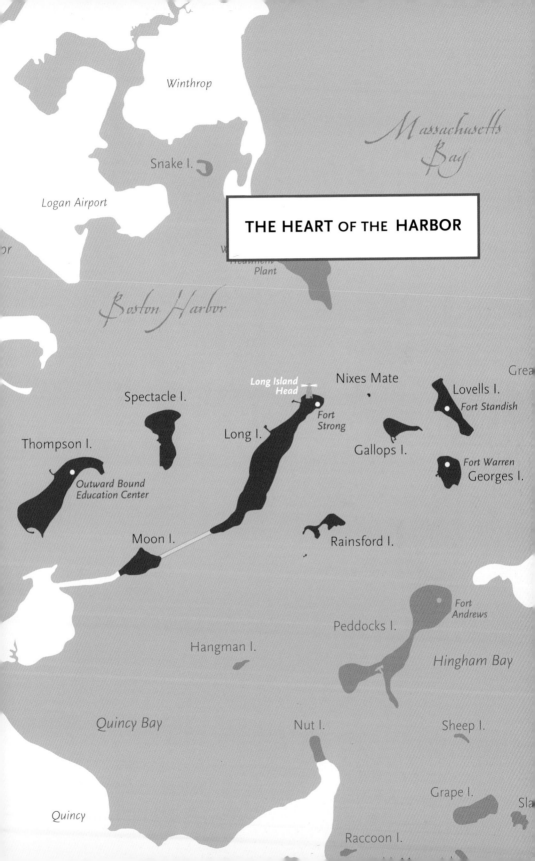

Winthrop

Massachusetts Bay

Snake I.

Logan Airport

or

THE HEART OF THE HARBOR

W

Treatment
Plant

Boston Harbor

Long Island
Head

Nixes Mate

Grea

Spectacle I.

Lovells I.
Fort Standish

Long I.

Fort
Strong

Thompson I.

Gallops I.

Fort Warren
Georges I.

Outward Bound
Education Center

Moon I.

Rainsford I.

Peddocks I.

Fort
Andrews

Hangman I.

Hingham Bay

Quincy Bay

Nut I.

Sheep I.

Grape I.

Sla

Quincy

Raccoon I.

Georges Island

With its labyrinth of dimly lit passageways, underground dungeons, spooky tunnels, and a drawbridge spanning a dry moat, mighty and historic Fort Warren on Georges Island may be the most visited attraction on the harbor islands. Though it was active from the 1850s through World War II, Fort Warren's most notable role came when it served as a prison for Confederate soldiers during the Civil War. Now an important National Historic Landmark, a visit to Fort Warren promises a fascinating, hands-on lesson in history and a ghost story worthy of a good campfire.

Originally known as Pemberton Island (after James Pemberton of Hull, who owned and farmed the island in the seventeenth century), the island was rechristened Georges Island by 1710. According to some accounts, the island took its new name from Boston merchant John George, Jr., who may have owned land on the island and was likely the same merchant who petitioned the Massachusetts legislature to build Boston Light in 1713.

One of Georges Island's first military moments came during the Revolutionary War, when a large earthwork (a fortification made by altering the landscape) was built in 1778 on the eastern side of the island. At the time, the French fleet was anchored in the harbor for repairs, and the earthwork defended them against the British navy, which was still lurking about Boston Harbor even though they had evacuated on March 17, 1776.

The British may have lost America during the Revolutionary War, but thirty-odd years later they managed to successfully cripple Boston's commerce with a naval blockade during the War of 1812. As a result, the United States military decided to upgrade its fortifications along the Eastern seaboard, and the federal government acquired the island for coastal defense in 1825. Because of its strategic location at the throat of the Narrows—the city's main shipping channel until the twentieth century—Georges Island was a natural choice as the site for the new fort.

Top: Union Officers. Below: Confederate Prisoners. From the collection of the New York Historical Society.

By 1825, however, heavy erosion and the sale of sand and gravel to passing ships in need of ballast had diminished Georges Island to half of its original size. The first act taken by the federal government after it purchased the island, therefore, was to build a massive seawall to protect it from further disappearing. By 1833, construction on the fort began in earnest. Fort Warren's ingenious (and very European) design was the brainchild of Sylvanus Thayer, an early superintendent of the United States Military Academy and known as "the Father of West Point." (Around Boston, he is also remembered as the namesake of Thayer Academy in Braintree.) Though the fort was neither attacked nor ever required to fire its cannons, Thayer's design, which incorporated impenetrable oak doors, portcullises, and a tremendous amount of armament, ensured it would have been ready. The fort was named in honor of Dr. Joseph Warren, a patriot hero at the Battle of Bunker Hill—though the name was actually transferred from an existing fort on Governor's Island, which eventually vanished from the map when it was incorporated into Logan Airport.

It would take decades for teams of stonemasons, carpenters, blacksmiths, and other laborers to complete this massive construction project, which was constantly plagued by delays in appropriations and a lack of skilled labor. (Not an entirely unfamiliar saga to present-day Bostonians.) When the military originally purchased Georges Island, it was composed of two drumlins, a topography similar to the East Head of Peddocks Island. Though the design of the fort took advantage of the island's landscape by incorporating the two hills into earthwork protection for the fort, some resculpting had to occur. Lowering and moving these hills in order to accommodate the fort was a considerable task, especially since the work was done by hand, using 536 picks and shovels and 406 wheelbarrows. Moving the granite blocks used to build the fort's twelve-foot-thick foundation walls was no easy feat either. Quarried at Cape Ann and Quincy, the granite blocks were unloaded onto carts at the island's dock, pulled uphill by oxen, and lifted into place by large derricks. It took so long to build Fort Warren that by the time the Civil War began, the fort was still not fully functional, and its defensive design was considered virtually obsolete.

Union soldiers stationed at Fort Warren during the early days of the war are credited with composing the lyrics to the famous marching song, *John Brown's Body*, which was sung to a tune from an old Methodist revivalist hymn that began, "Say, brothers, will you meet us?" According to some accounts, the song may not have been originally composed to honor the "real" John Brown, the famed abolitionist leader who raided Harper's Ferry, but to poke fun at a solider at Fort Warren who shared the same name. Regardless, the men of the Massachusetts Infantry who trained at

Fort Warren carried the song with them into battle, and its popularity quickly spread through the Union ranks. The rhythm and memorable chorus of *John Brown's Body* made it a natural marching song. When Julia Ward Howe heard Union troops singing the song while marching into battle, she was inspired to write an alternative set of lyrics. Those words, combined with the original melody, became an American anthem: *The Battle Hymn of the Republic*.

A little more than six months after the first shots were fired at Fort Sumter, the federal government decided to transport Confederate prisoners to Fort Warren, which was under the command of Colonel Justin Dimick. The veteran officer was told to ready the fort for the arrival of 150 prisoners, so he was understandably shocked when, on Halloween in 1861, a boatload of more than eight hundred men docked at the island. Fort Warren was overrun and ill-prepared, which resulted in food rations and prisoners sleeping on floors. A newspaper account from November 1861 reported that when the prisoners arrived at Fort Warren "pity rather than the hatred of the visitors was

JAY SCHMIDT ON FORT WARREN

Ever since Jay Schmidt first visited Fort Warren as a young boy in 1957, he was fascinated by the fort and its history. That curiosity spurred him to spend years researching and writing a book on the fort. Jay talks about his first trip to Fort Warren and his favorite story from its rich history:

"My friend's father was a pilot on a Boston fire boat, and they did harbor cruises on Sundays to inspect facilities. He invited my father, my two brothers, and me to go out to Georges Island. I had no idea there was even a fort out there. At that time, it was in disrepair. The parade ground had not been mown in years—the grass was three feet high—and every room we went into had broken-down timbers and piles of lumber all over the floor. But I was fascinated by the fort and by the stories the caretaker told us. He mentioned Mason and Slidell, and we had just studied them in school. We had such a good time running around the fort and ever since then, I've always been interested in what went on there.

"My favorite story about Fort Warren is the one about the four Confederate prisoners who escaped in 1863 near the sallyport. They slipped out through one of the musketry loopholes and went up and over the coverface. But it turns out the night was too windy and rough to swim off the island, so they had to go back inside the fort, climbing up a rope they had left hanging from the loophole. They waited a couple of nights for the weather to clear, and they escaped again. Two of them were captured in the bushes, but the other two successfully sailed over to Lovells on a large pine board target. The ones who escaped were eventually captured by a revenue cutter near Portland, Maine, and returned to the fort."

excited by the sad spectacle." Bostonians responded by donating food, beds, and other supplies to assist the Confederate prisoners, hoping that proper treatment of the prisoners might inspire equal compassion toward Union prisoners of war. Additionally, these acts of generosity bolstered the moral high ground of abolitionists.

The most prominent prisoners held at Fort Warren were James Mason and John Slidell, who arrived within a month of the first prisoners. The capture of Mason and Slidell, who were dispatched by Confederate President Jefferson Davis to Europe on a diplomatic mission, provoked the international incident now known as the Trent Affair. The pair were intercepted by Union troops and captured aboard the British mail steamer *Trent*. The British, outraged that one of their ships had been boarded by Union troops, put their fleet on notice, and demanded that the two Confederate commissioners be released from Fort Warren. President Lincoln feared a rift with the British and eventually acquiesced, releasing Mason and Slidell on New Year's Day in 1862.

Other notable Confederate figures detained at Fort Warren were former Kentucky Governor Charles Morehead, Baltimore Mayor George William Brown, General Simon Bolivar Buckner, and Alexander Hamilton Stephens, the vice president of the Confederacy. While life for the prisoners varied depending on their status, rank, and wealth, conditions were never that severe. Indeed, many prisoners praised

Dimick for his kindness and humane treatment. When the orders were received in March 1862 to direct Buckner to solitary confinement, Dimick was reportedly so distressed that he wept while conveying the order—and was ultimately consoled by Buckner himself, a Confederate general! Dimick garnered so much respect that both Union and Confederate officers served as pallbearers at his funeral in 1871.

Wealthier political prisoners and officers were allowed to supply themselves with whatever luxuries they could afford and make arrangements to buy. More regulations were enforced as the war went on, but in its infancy, prisoners were allowed to receive newspapers, letters, gifts, and even alcohol. When weather permitted, they were allowed outside the doors of their quarters to congregate, walk, or have a smoke.

Only thirteen Confederate prisoners out of the hundreds and hundreds who passed through the gates of Fort Warren died on the island, and none were killed by Union troops. In fact, the only recorded executions that occurred on Fort Warren were of two deserters from the Union army: Charles Carpenter and Matthew Riley, "bounty jumpers" who would repeatedly enlist in units to collect a cash bounty, desert, and then join another unit under an assumed name to collect another bounty. They were captured, convicted by a court-martial, and killed by a military firing squad on April 22, 1864.

Of course, if you were to ask anyone familiar with Georges Island what its most enduring story is, they would respond by telling you about "The Lady in Black." Popularized by historian Edward Rowe Snow, this tale is now an essential part of the island's fabric.

According to the legend, the wife of a Confederate prisoner, dressed as a man and brandishing a pistol, snuck into the fort in an attempt to free her newlywed husband. She succeeded in reaching her husband's cell, but as they tried to escape the dungeon, Union troops discovered their scheme and notified Colonel Dimick. When the colonel came upon the pair, the wife fired at Dimick, but her gun exploded and killed her husband instead. Dimick had no choice but to order the woman to hang as a spy. Before her execution, she requested that she be properly dressed in women's clothing. She was given black robes and hanged from the gallows.

From the Civil War through the Second World War, many a soldier stationed on the parapets claimed to see the frightening ghost of the Lady in Black, who is said to prowl through the fort's many passageways to this day. As far back as January 1862, the *Gloucester Telegraph* reported that sentinels keeping midnight rounds saw a spiritual phenomena near some of the rebel graves. The soldiers reported spying the image of an old woman "vindictively frisking about the ruins of an old building from which she was ejected some time previous to her death." Whether or not Georges Island has a resident ghost is hard to verify, of course, but one thing is for certain—a possible sighting of the Lady in Black was as good excuse as any when it came to getting out of a monotonous night of guard duty.

The fort remained active through the Spanish-American War, World War I, and World War II, and was increasingly fortified with more powerful guns. During the world wars, Fort Warren was used to monitor and control the mines planted in the southern part of Boston Harbor. After World War II, and with the onset of the atomic age, Fort Warren was rendered militarily useless and abandoned. Georges Island was considered as the location for a toxic waste dump in the 1950s, but thanks in part to the efforts of Edward Rowe Snow, those plans were thwarted. Today, a memorial to Snow graces the island he helped to popularize and save, and a shade shelter bears his name.

Georges Island's scenic picnic grounds, open fields, and gravel beach draw as many visitors as Fort Warren itself. Along with Spectacle Island, Georges Island is the most-visited island in the harbor chain. It is a thirty-minute ferry ride from Long Wharf in Boston, and visitors can transfer there for inter-island ferry service to Lovells, Peddocks, Grape, and Bumpkin Islands.

Throughout the summer, Georges Island offers a wide variety of public programs such as Civil War reenactments and old-time baseball games. On Fridays during the summer, kids will enjoy watching and participating in the plays performed by City Stage Co. In September, the Boston Harbor Islands Regatta—a wonderful outdoor festival as much as a boat race—is held on Georges Island.

Guided tours of Fort Warren are available daily, and a new visitor center brings the history of Fort Warren, its prisoners and enlisted men, and Boston's coastal defenses to life with interactive exhibits and a short film. Another wonderful addition to Georges Island is the new outpost of Jasper White's Summer Shack, where you can enjoy lobster rolls or any type of fried seafood you'd like under a covered pavilion with views of the Boston skyline. On the hill behind the Summer Shack stands a marker erected by the United Daughters of the Confederacy with the names of the thirteen Confederate soldiers who died while in captivity at Fort Warren.

A pathway leading up from the dock goes by the fort's guard house, underneath a tunnel in the coverface, and to the sallyport. A wooden bridge crosses the dry moat, and leads visitors through the fort's original oak doors. The expansive parade ground unfolds as you pass through the sallyport. This field provided space for infantry training and inspections as well as off-duty activities such as baseball games. During wartime, the parade ground was used for temporary support buildings and tents to house additional troops. A granite powder magazine is the only permanent building on the parade ground.

Staircases lead to the grass-covered ramparts, which offer great views of Boston and the neighboring islands. The emplacements for the fort's massive guns can still be seen along the ramparts. The two biggest guns, 12-inch rifles on disappearing carriages, were located in Battery Stevenson, which was completed in 1902.

The bastions on the ground level, filled with dramatic arches and vaulted roofs, will thrill photographers. Visitors can walk through the fort's old bakery, living quarters, and hospital. During the summer, beams of light stream through the narrow musket loops onto the brick walls and wood floors. Children especially love to explore the fort's nooks, crannies, and winding corridors—but keep an eye on them, as some areas have steep drop-offs and hidden hazards.

Toward the end of the day, as the shadows grow long and the sun sinks over Boston, the throngs of visitors to Fort Warren begin to leave on the ferries and the atmosphere of this impressive citadel changes. Soon, you may be all alone. The hallways in front of you begin to fade into the gloaming. The wind begins to howl and the floors creak. A pigeon's flapping wings echo through the empty chambers, and a startling shiver will run down your spine. All around you, the history and legends of Fort Warren coalesce. But if you pay attention, you just might catch a glimpse of something—or someone—from the corner of your eye.

ADDITIONAL INFORMATION

S Rangers provide guided tours of Fort Warren. The Island Alliance schedules family events on summer weekends. Visit: www.harborislands.org

🎭 Performances by City Stage Co. are held on Fridays from late June until late August, usually beginning at 11:30 AM and again at 1:00 PM (times may change). All shows are designed for children.

⚓ Secure moorings are available off Georges Island through the Spectacle Island Marina. Call: 857-452-7221 or hail the Spectacle Island Marina on VHF 69. Reservations are advised.

Private boaters may use the dock at Georges Island on a first-come, first-serve basis.

Spectacle Island

The view from the grassy summit of the north drumlin of Spectacle Island is itself a spectacle to behold. All of metropolitan Boston unfolds before you in a breathtaking, unobstructed 360-degree panorama. Castle Island and Pleasure Bay in South Boston appear as though they are right beneath your feet. And even though it's over five miles away, it seems as though you could reach out and pluck the Prudential Center from the city skyline. From this vantage point the harbor activity is astonishing. Each sailboat, tanker, tug, and motorboat proclaims the vitality of this maritime city.

Now, turn to the other side of this 157-foot-high perch, where the constellation of islands is perfectly laid out across the shimmering surface of the harbor. In the foreground, Thompson, Long, and Moon Islands stretch across the water. Beyond Long Island, Boston Light is perfectly framed by Gallops and Lovells. And in the distance, the Brewsters point the way toward the open sea. On clear days, you can see up the coast forty miles to the north. This is the highest point in Boston Harbor—a good sixty-eight feet higher than Boston Light.

Such a majestic view is a fitting crown for this jewel in the harbor's island necklace. To take in this vista today is to overlook the fact that you are standing atop eighty feet of trash and a legacy of environmental neglect that, unfortunately, was typical of the way Bostonians treated their harbor and its islands. For decades, Spectacle Island was a wasteland, home to a variety of sordid functions, including a city landfill, horse rendering factory, and quarantine station.

Now, after nearly fifteen years of environmental cleanup and a cost of more than $170 million, Spectacle Island has been transformed into a 105-acre recreation area, the showpiece of the Boston Harbor Islands national park area. Opened in 2006, the new park includes five miles of walking trails, a marina, swimming beaches, fishing, and an environmentally friendly visitor center. The remarkable renewal of Spectacle Island from a smoldering dump to a public park is representative of the rebirth of the Boston Harbor Islands as a whole.

Formed when glaciers left behind deposits of sand, gravel, rubble, and debris, Spectacle Island has been a "dumping ground" from the beginning. Those deposits produced the island's two drumlins, which the Massachusett tribe, who summered there for thousands of years, referred to as "The Twins." Archaeologists have excavated middens—piles of clam shells and other refuse discarded by Native Americans—that date back 1,500 years. Other artifacts found by archaeologists include pottery shards, stone arrowheads, and tools.

When the first European settlers arrived, the two drumlins of the island were connected by a sandbar so narrow that it was submerged by large tidal surges. The colonists came to call this place Spectacle Island because its shape resembled that of

The view from the summit of Spectacle Island.

a pair of eyeglasses. The Massachusetts Bay Colony granted Spectacle Island—along with Deer, Hog, and Long Islands—to the town of Boston in the 1630s. The yearly rent for all four islands was a total of four shillings. The town rented the land for sixpence an acre to pay for free schools in the new settlement, and the Puritans used the island to graze cattle and harvest lumber for firewood and shipbuilding.

In 1717, Spectacle Island became a makeshift quarantine station, "for the reception and entertainment of sick persons coming from beyond the sea, in order to prevent the spreading of infection." The quarantine station was often used for early Irish immigrants thought to be carrying smallpox, measles, or other contagious diseases. Twenty years after the quarantine station was established on Spectacle Island, it was moved to Rainsford Island, and land use returned to agriculture.

By the 1840s, yachtsmen and Bostonians on pleasure excursions discovered the island anew. Vacationers in search of fun flocked to the two summer resorts that opened on the island. It appears, however, that the fun might have been a touch too lively for some. One Sunday in 1856, police arrested a party of about twenty-five men disembarking at Long Wharf after a boat trip to Spectacle Island. The authorities seized a roulette table, cards, and dice, and these wayward gentlemen were charged with gambling on the boat and the island. Apparently, such nefarious boat trips had become too popular a pastime for a city founded by Puritans, particularly on the Sabbath. Shortly after the police crackdown, the island's hotels ceased operation.

With the resorts gone, Spectacle Island was sold in 1857 to Boston businessman Nahum Ward, who moved his industrial operations offshore to the island. Over the next hundred years, Ward's factories and the subsequent uses of the island would plague surrounding communities with noxious odors that were often far stronger than the salty ocean breeze. Among the plants built by N. Ward & Co. on the island was a horse rendering operation. In reality, this was a small—albeit colorful—part of Ward's overall operations, staffed by three or four men out of the sixty he employed, but it was this aspect of Ward's business that earned the island the nickname "Boney Wards."

As unpalatable as it may seem by today's standards, Ward's disposal of two thousand or more dead horses a year was a necessary evil that helped prevent a public health epidemic in Boston. The company's horse hearses were familiar sights passing along the city streets of Boston, collecting carcasses free of charge. Prior to Ward's company, which was established in 1828, the custom was to throw the dead horses directly into the harbor. Occasionally, the horses were towed out into the open sea only to float back in, becoming entangled in the fingers of the city's wharves or washing onto the shores of the harbor islands.

Once collected, the carcasses were then taken to Ward's wharf where the manes were sheared and placed in a loft to dry. The hair would be steamed, cleansed, and curled and would later be used as mattress and furniture stuffing. Each evening a barge with the horses would sail to Spectacle Island. At the factory, the skins were

Though unpalatable, Nahum Ward's horse rendering plant provided a vital service to the city of Boston, as this 1906 photograph of the produce center in Faneuil Hall demonstrates. Courtesy the Library of Congress.

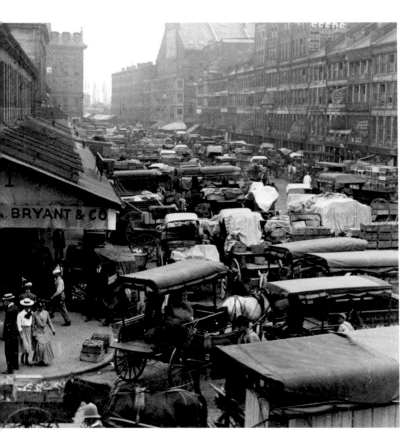

removed, salted, and prepared for sale to manufacturers of fine upholstery and high-end shoe makers. One year, all the skins were used to make baseballs, perhaps an early indication of Boston's obsession. From the remaining carcasses the factory extracted oils and produced fertilizer. And, yes, the hooves were used for glue. The factory also took in twenty to thirty tons of beef scraps each day. These scraps would be pressed into cakes, mixed with other ingredients, and eventually made into dog biscuits. (Distressingly, before the Civil War, the cakes were used to feed slaves as well.) Thankfully, all that remains of Ward's Spectacle Island operations today are the four granite piers at the base of the north drumlin.

Given the unpleasant nature of Ward's business, it's hard to imagine that Ward's employees actually lived on the island. Upwards of fifteen of those employees raised their families there, too. (Families continued to live on Spectacle well into the 1950s.) Perhaps even harder to imagine is that many of the children raised on Spectacle

Island considered it paradise. For them, the island provided the wonderful adventure of rural life in clear sight of the city's skyline.

To educate the children of Spectacle Island, the city of Boston established its smallest school. This simple, red, one-room structure could have been ripped from the pages of *Little House on the Prairie*—except that it was located on an island of factories right off the shore of an urban metropolis. The children attended the school until the eighth grade when they were either sent to schools in Boston or put to work on the island. The factory provided the building and furniture, while the city paid for books, stationery, and a teacher, who would either stay on the island while school was in session or travel to the island daily by towboat.

Ward's factories caused a powerful stench, but residents downwind of Spectacle Island found little relief after the operations closed. In the early 1900s Spectacle Island became home to a grease reclamation facility and disposal plant that would

This photograph, taken in 1909 South Boston, demonstrates the disregard with which Boston's waterfront was treated over the years. Courtesy the Library of Congress.

convert garbage into various marketable byproducts such as soap and fertilizer. A few years later, the island became a landfill, and the city's garbage was shipped to the island until 1959. By the time the dump closed, the trash was eighty-five feet deep, adding an additional thirty-seven acres to the footprint of Spectacle Island. So deep was the refuse that a bulldozer supposedly sunk into it in the 1950s, never to be found again.

The garbage dump was an assault on the senses. Spontaneous methane combustions commonly lit up the night sky. Depending on the wind, the overwhelming smell could be detected at the Farm School on Thompson Island, the City Point section of South

Boston, Winthrop, and even as far north as Swampscott. The odor was particularly pungent during the summer, forcing residents to shutter their windows on the hottest and most oppressive days of the year. It is said that the smell was so bad that in foggy weather ships could

get their bearings simply by the stench emanating from Spectacle Island.

In the same year the dump closed, Spectacle Island became the backdrop for another sordid tale—this time a murder mystery followed by a sensational trial that captured the attention of the United States and the world. In September 1959, a tugboat captain discovered the beaten body of twenty-three-year-old divorcee Lynn Kauffman washed up on the island's shore, clad only in Bermuda shorts and blue slippers. Kauffman had been aboard the Dutch passenger freighter *Utrecht* that had just completed a forty-four-day voyage from Singapore and was sailing to New York City. The ship's handsome (and married) radio officer, Willem van Rie, had been carrying on a torrid affair with Kauffman and, following twenty hours of questioning, admitted to striking her the night of her disappearance. Even though he immediately recanted, police charged him with murder.

The radio officer stood trial in Suffolk Superior Court in Boston, and van Rie took

to the stand in his own defense, proclaiming his innocence. There was no sign of violence in Kauffman's cabin, and witnesses testified that they heard Kauffman in her cabin at seven o'clock the night of her disappearance, at which point the ship was seven or eight miles distant from Spectacle Island. The harbormaster testified that there was no way the current could have swept Kauffman onto the island from that far offshore. The jury acquitted van Rie, and the mystery was never solved. Were the witnesses mistaken? Had she committed suicide? Did she accidentally fall overboard? Or did van Rie—or another passenger—get away with murder?

The media spotlight eventually faded, but Spectacle's squalid conditions persisted far longer. For decades after the landfill closed, Spectacle Island was not only a visible eyesore, but also a cancer, leeching toxins and pollutants into Boston Harbor.

Through a triumph of imagination and engineering acumen, the problem of Spectacle Island was solved by yet another challenge: what to do with all the fill excavated from Boston's Big Dig. In a marriage of Boston's two biggest public works projects of the last century—the Central Artery Tunnel Project and the harbor cleanup—the excavated material from the Ted Williams Tunnel and other roadways was used to cap and close the landfill, resculpting Spectacle Island. As luck would have it, the Big Dig has not only contributed to the revitalization of the harbor by reconnecting Boston's waterfront to the rest of the city, it has led to the rebirth of this jewel of the Boston Harbor Islands.

In many ways, the project was a throwback to Boston's centuries-old practice of adding fill to its rivers and harbor to expand its footprint and create new neighborhoods, such as the Back Bay. The first bargeload of excavated material made the trip to Spectacle Island in 1992. Over the next five years, barge after barge made that same journey, eventually transporting 3.5 million cubic yards of clay, dirt, dredged material, and gravel that would smother the landfill under countless tons of mud. So much fill was added that both drumlins increased by sixty feet in height.

Once the landfill was closed, two to five feet of topsoil were added and 2,400 trees and 26,000 shrubs were planted. Native and non-native species that thrive in sandy

The restoration of Spectacle Island using excavated material from the Big Dig was an extraordinary feat of engineering. The tricky logistics of converting an abandoned landfill to a park were made even more extreme by the landfill's island location. Ron Killian, Chris Barnett, and Ralph DeGregorio of the Central Artery/Tunnel Project give some insight into the complexities of this massive project.

"The entire Spectacle Island project was highly unusual. Landfills that do get restored are not usually islands, so the biggest challenge we faced was building by water. Everything on that island needed to get there by boat—including 3.5 million cubic yards of fill. We had to have a dedicated boating facility on the South Boston side. We had to have barges. We had to have tugs on standby. And all the labor needed to be transported to the island. It was a huge operation. Plus, we had to work under additional environmental requirements and permitting commitments because the site was in the middle of the harbor.

"Virtually no blade of grass was on the island before restoration started. We had to completely wipe the slate clean and rebuild from scratch. And that's something that doesn't hit you when you visit the island today. We built beaches around a third of the perimeter of the island. When we started the project, the 'beaches' on Spectacle were basically eroding trash. We dredged everything up, and put down stone and sand, so the beach you see today is almost completely artificial.

"There was a lot of thought given to the landscaping of the island. We were concerned about sustainability. We selected species for wind, salt, and drought tolerance. And, of course, we were concerned with resistance to disease. We didn't want the island to be a monoculture that could be wiped out by one bug. We also looked at animal habitats, and what shrubbery would provide cover and food for birds. We wanted tree species that weren't going to topple, as the soil doesn't have much depth to it because it's a landfill cap. By now, the trees are pretty established and are likely going to make it.

"The same consideration was given to the seawalls. When people go around the island they say: These are some seawalls! What were they thinking? And what we were thinking was a storm surge, high tides, and waves."

soil, salty air, and harsh wind and sun were chosen. No deep-rooted species that might pierce the cap were planted. Meadow grasses on the sides of the drumlins help maintain the stability of the slopes and dominate the landscape, at least until the deciduous and evergreen trees mature. Vents sprinkled across the island allow methane underneath the ground to escape safely, and the landfill cap is constantly monitored to ensure it is intact. A seawall fourteen feet thick helps prevent the seepage of toxins into the harbor and protects the coastline against erosion.

It is a wonderful quirk of fate that what used to be the most environmentally degraded island in Boston Harbor is now its most environmentally friendly. (Although

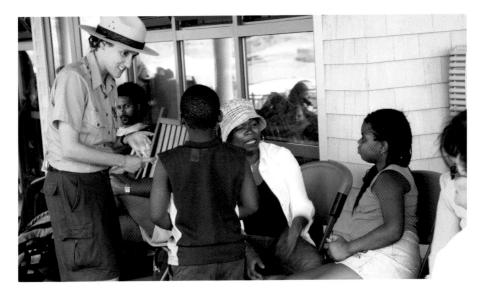

it should be noted that Spectacle Island displays a tradition of recycling, from the horse-rendering operations to the grease reclamation plant to the use of Big Dig leftovers.) The benches and picnic tables on Spectacle Island are made from recycled materials. Solar panels resting on the south-facing roof of the visitor center supply enough power for the center and the island's small fleet of electrical vehicles. Water used in the center's kitchen and sinks is collected, filtered, and used to irrigate flowers. There are modern composting toilets that use no water or chemicals. By all accounts, Spectacle Island is authentically *green*.

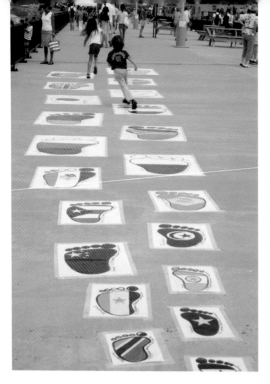

As one of the hub islands, and just fifteen minutes from downtown Boston, Spectacle Island offers a wide array of recreational opportunities not to be missed. Sand was imported to create a popular swimming beach complete with rinse stations and changing facilities. The marina includes thirty-eight boat slips, and private boaters can stay overnight, enjoying music on the pier and bonfires on the beach. (The marina supplies the marshmallows.) And lest you think Spectacle offers nothing but lazy days on the beach, summertime brings Sunday jazz concerts, guided tours, and a slew of public programming for children. Birders can spot upwards of one hundred different species, such as bobolinks, warblers, and Savannah Sparrows; and anglers, who are often seen at the end of the dock, say the stripers, cod, and flounder are among the fish biting.

The walking trails on Spectacle Island provide both easy strolls and vigorous climbs. Gravel pathways carved into the north and south drumlins wind their way to the summits. Atop the peaks are picnic areas and charming gazebos. Wayfaring signs include historical vignettes about the island's past, and, in the late summer and early fall, migrating monarch butterflies flutter among the wildflowers along the trails.

The Summer Shack, local celebrity chef Jasper White's popular eatery, offers tasty treats and hosts authentic New England clambakes at sunset on the pier each Thursday during the summer. The visitor center also has restrooms and exhibits about island history, but the best part is outside, under the porch. There, a long row of rocking chairs look out on the harbor and city skyline. If you happen to find yourself relaxing in one of those chairs during a concert, you'll find that the sense of renewal exuded by this revitalized island can reach into a visitor's soul.

Sunday jazz concerts on Spectacle Island are a great way to spend the afternoon.

ADDITIONAL INFORMATION

The Island Alliance schedules family events on summer weekends. Log onto www.harborislands.org for listings. For more information on Jasper White's sunset clambakes, visit www.spectacleclambake.com.

Ranger-led tours of the island leave from the visitor center. Rangers also lead kayak trips for beginners around the island's cove

Fishing poles and nets are available at the visitor center.

Marina reservations can be made by contacting Spectacle Island Marina at 857-452-7221 or hailing VHF 69.

Lovells Island

From the southern beach of Lovells Island, the shoreline of Georges Island seems so close it's hard to imagine that for centuries the waterway between them was the lone shipping lane into Boston. Particularly at low tide, it's easy to see how deadly shipwrecks on Lovells Island were once a fairly common occurrence. The Narrows, as it's known, is a rocky passage, only a quarter mile from shore to shore and with a channel no more than two hundred yards wide. For large ships and big ocean steamers making their way to Boston's port, the trip by Lovells Island was no easier than threading a needle.

If you think driving the narrow, crooked streets of downtown Boston is hair-raising, consider plotting a course through its harbor: The islands that bless Boston Harbor were (and can be) a curse to negotiate even under the best conditions. Before the modern-day benefits of GPS and detailed nautical charts, captains were forced to contend with hidden shoals, powerful currents, and the sheer volume of sailing vessels. The names of harbor landmarks—Hypocrite Channel, Devil's Back, and the Roaring Bulls—in no way belie the peril that faced ships in the final ten miles of their journey. Tiptoeing through the precarious approach to reach the safety of the deep inner harbor was tricky enough for experienced pilots, let alone for those seeing it for the first time.

The real danger came from unpredictable weather that could quickly transform conditions from placid to fierce. Many a boat has been lost in the fog or blown ashore by a howling Nor'easter. During the winter, frozen sea spray could encrust a ship in ice, making it impossible to work the sails. The skeletons of hundreds of ships litter the floor of Boston Harbor and are testament to its difficult passage.

A number of these ships met their end on Lovells Island, in plain sight of the city. How terrifying it must have been for those survivors shipwrecked on Lovells, particularly during the winter when they had to endure bitter winds through the darkness of night. And how frustrating it must have been to be so close to safety—with the warm, alabaster glow of Boston in the distance—but too far for anyone to know they were there?

One of the most notable shipwrecks on Lovells Island was that of the 74-gun French warship *Magnifique*. In 1782, during the waning days of the American Revolution, the ship ran aground on the western side of the island while trying to navigate the Narrows. Although he may have been a bit of a scapegoat, David Darling, the Boston pilot of the *Magnifique,* never lived down the mistake. He later became a church sexton and an undertaker—fitting, perhaps, for someone who sent a ship to its watery grave. It is said that neighborhood children would rib Darling by chalking the church doors with the lines, "Don't you run this ship ashore, as you did the seventy-four!"

Darling's error and the subsequent wreck had considerable implications for American history. Fearing a rift with their major ally, the Americans presented France with the 74-gun USS *America* as compensation—even though the vessel had been promised to naval hero John Paul Jones, who'd diligently supervised its construction. Without an American ship to command, the Father of the American Navy traveled to France and eventually entered into the service of the Russian navy under Catherine the Great. To this day, treasure hunters continue to be lured to the shoals of Lovells Island by the dream of recovering the gold and silver coins said to be aboard the *Magnifique*.

Four years after the *Magnifique* wrecked, a tragic fate befell a packet ship from Maine. One dark December night during a blizzard, the ship ran aground on the rocks of Ram's Head, a bar extending off the northern side of the island. All thirteen passengers and crew managed to make it to shore, but the elements were simply too harsh. Without shelter, the survivors eventually died of exposure. When found the following morning, it is said that a young couple engaged to be married was found dead in each other's arms, huddled behind a boulder in their desperate quest for survival. The rock, located on the western side of the island, was dubbed "Lovers' Rock."

The author of the first American bestseller, Susanna Rowson, was aboard yet another ship that wrecked on Lovells Island. In January 1767, four-year-old Rowson was traveling with her father, a British revenue officer transferring to the port of Boston. The ship ran aground at night, and the sea encased it in ice. Luckily, everyone onboard was saved by fishermen living on Lovells. Twenty-three years later, Rowson wrote the novel *Charlotte Temple,* the biggest-selling book in the United States until *Uncle Tom's Cabin*; but it was Rowson's subsequent book, *Rebecca,* which drew from her horrific experience on Lovells Island.

The spate of shipwrecks off Lovells Island led to the construction of the first hut of refuge in the United States by the Massachusetts Humane Society in 1787. The small red hut on the Narrows side of the island offered salvation in the form of dry clothing, food, blankets, wood, and a flint and tinder to kindle a fire. No sooner was the hut built than it was credited with saving the lives of six people whose shallop bound for Cape Ann wrecked off Lovells' coast. A similar hut was built on the east end of Lovells in 1789. Scores of comparable structures would arise along the Massachusetts coast in following years, and the hut was part of the first organized life-saving efforts in North America and a precursor of the United States Coast Guard. The frequent shipwrecks in Boston Harbor also gave rise to a proud tradition of lifesaving among brave volunteers from Hull who saved hundreds of people from distressed ships.

At the turn of the twentieth century a second entrance to Boston Harbor was dredged through Broad Sound, and a pair of range lights was constructed on Lovells Island to guide mariners through the new shipping channel. The range lights, located on the northern side of the island, stood until they were torn down in 1939 so that the military could use the land as a rifle range. The only surviving structure from the range lights is the dilapidated shell of the old oil house, which was used to store the fuel that lit the beacons.

Now the primary entrance for deep-draft ships, the channel through Broad Sound increased the strategic importance of Lovells Island, as the island was flanked by the harbor's two principal openings. As a result, the federal government in 1900 added the island to the growing list of military sites peppering the harbor. Named in honor of the Pilgrim Miles Standish, Fort Standish served Boston from the Spanish-American War all the way through World War II. Although Fort Standish was only a lightly manned sub-post of Fort Warren during the Spanish-American War, it was fully garrisoned in World War I. Between the world wars, Fort Standish was placed on caretaker status, but it was reactivated for World War II, at which time it had sixty structures.

Left: The old parade grounds on Lovells Island make for a unique campsite.
Right: Tide pools provide hands-on discovery, and looking across Black Rock Channel toward Graves Light at low tide.

The numerous ruins of Fort Standish, abandoned in the late 1940s, are sure to delight those interested in military history. Most striking are the hulking gun batteries. Though they are now crumbling and obsolete, these batteries, along with the cracking asphalt roads, stand testament to the island's days as a military installation. Today, these roads have been reinvented as hiking trails, and the walk along the east side of the island leads to Battery Burbeck-Morris. This towering battery emerges suddenly and the concrete staircase leading to the top of the battery has the desolate feel of an Aztec temple.

Battery Burbeck-Morris, cut into the central drumlin, once held 10-inch rifles with a range of nine miles, firing over earthen parapets before recoiling out of sight. The guns were dismounted in 1943. For those who aren't intimidated by heights, walk along the top of the parapets for excellent views of the outer harbor. (Some staircases to the top of the battery lack railings, so use caution.)

Walking counterclockwise around Lovells Island, the trail north of Battery Burbeck-Morris ends amid white sand dunes and wispy grasses. Continuing north along the shore of Broad Sound, the island begins to narrow. The area surrounding the oil house is carpeted with mussel shells, washed ashore from the flats of Broad Sound. North of the oil house is a salt marsh and heavily wooded area that is more difficult to traverse. At the northern tip of Lovells Island are the remains of Battery Terrill.

If the east side of the island has you thinking you've discovered Aztec ruins, the west side of the island will give you a more apocalyptic feel, eerily reminiscent to the finale of *Planet of the Apes*. The beach leads past the ruins of massive searchlight platforms that have collapsed from the eroding bluff above. Near the old dock, enormous pieces of rubble from the fort's World War I compound are partially exposed.

Continue south toward the present-day pier and you'll come across a long stretch of sand dunes and staghorn sumac groves. Near the pier is the remnant of a lookout tower perched on four concrete pillars. Through the narrow lookout slot, military men once took measurements to help aim gun and mortar batteries.

Campsites for both groups and individuals are scattered across Lovells Island—though one of the most unique settings has to be on the south side of the island, in the old parade grounds. During the summer the parade grounds are filled with tents, hemmed in by the concrete ruins of Battery Whipple and Battery Williams. Battery Whipple held two 6-inch guns with a range of nine miles. Battery Williams, built in the early 1900s, mounted 3-inch rapid fire guns with a range of just over five miles to protect both the Narrows and Broad Sound from possible attack. The emplacements below housed officer and gun crew day rooms, an equipment storehouse, and magazines.

Behind the two batteries on the island's southeastern tip, tidal pools teeming with sea-life thrive amid the remnants of the old seawall. It takes a little effort to scale the large

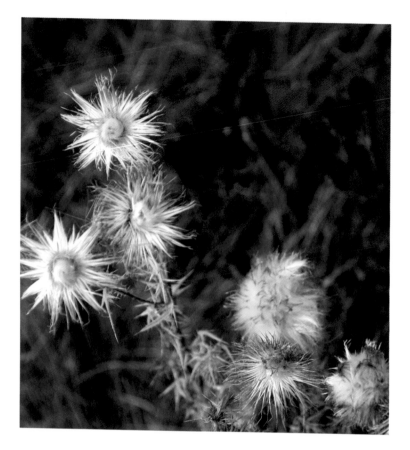

stones, but it provides a great location to watch the gulls scouting the pools for their next meal. It also offers a superb view of Boston Light on Little Brewster Island, the towering bluff on Great Brewster Island, Graves Light, and the open sea beyond.

Just north of the seawall—and directly across the island from the pier—is a long, sweeping beach that curves along Broad Sound. If you're planning to take a dip, the water in the Broad Sound is far more suitable for swimming than the swiftly moving currents along the Narrows; however, the beach along Broad Sound is rocky and not staffed by lifeguards.

While Spectacle Island is a better option for swimming, camping on Lovells is still popular due to its proximity to the city. However, the fog horns, planes, and party boats have been known to make the island a noisier choice as well. If you do camp on Lovells, be prepared to encounter the island's large population of European hares, introduced in the 1940s or 1950s, though no one is quite sure how or when the colony came to be. These rabbits are not a native species, and it's possible they were brought to the island by military personnel or a caretaker. They burrow warrens in the island's sandy soil, eat the staghorn sumac and sea grass, and like the party boats, they tend to come out when the sun is going down.

ADDITIONAL INFORMATION

S Ranger-led tours available.

🏕 Reservations are required to camp on Lovells Island and can be made online at www.ReserveAmerica.com or call toll-free 877-422-6762. Your camping reservation is not site specific. At check-in an island ranger will assign you a campsite. The camping season runs from late June to early September.

⚓ For boaters arriving by private craft, docks are for drop-off only.

🚢 To get to Lovells, take the free inter-island ferry from Georges Island. Consult crew onboard the mainland ferry. The inter-island ferry is also available from the Hingham Shipyard and Hull.

Gallops as seen from inside Fort Warren on Georges Island.

Gallops Island

Tucked away in the North End's Langone Park, stands a gray stone pedestal topped by a sinking ship and a band of Morse code. The monument honors the graduates of the Gallops Island Radio Training Station, who gave their lives aboard merchant ships supplying American forces during World War II.

This overlooked statue seems to symbolize the forgotten island where it once stood. Closed to the public for more than a decade, Gallops Island, which protected Boston from the double threats of disease and attack has begun to fade from Boston's collective consciousness.

Used by Native Americans for thousands of years, the island takes its name from Captain John Gallop, a noted Boston Harbor pilot who owned it along with Nixes Mate in the 1600s. Gallops Island's fertile land was used for agriculture into the early nineteenth century, and its farms often supplied ships anchored in Nantasket Roads with vegetables and other important staples.

But Gallops Island has a rich and unique military record as well. During the Revolutionary War, French troops protected the harbor by erecting earthen batteries and mounting cannons on the island's northern bluff. During the Civil War, as many as three thousand Union soldiers on their way to and from the warfront were quartered on the island. (Before receiving their final discharge and parading through the streets of Boston, the famed 54th Massachusetts Volunteer Infantry Regiment, immortalized in the film *Glory*, spent a number of days encamped on the island in the summer of 1865.)

After the Civil War, Boston moved its quarantine station from Deer Island to Gallops. Arriving immigrants were brought ashore Gallops Island, where they were forced to strip and scrub themselves with disinfectants. Between 1867 and 1937, several thousand immigrants as well as Bostonians believed to be afflicted with yellow fever, smallpox, cholera, and even leprosy were quarantined on the island, and approximately 250 people lay buried in an unmarked cemetery on the eastern end of the island.

While not the threat it was to colonial Boston, smallpox remained a dire concern to public health officials even at the dawn of the twentieth century. During the smallpox epidemic of May 1901, the city not only isolated the sick on Gallops Island but also offered free vaccinations to the healthy. Because there was still considerable reluctance to vaccination, the city ordered house-to-house vaccinations. Anyone who refused paid a five-dollar fine or served a fifteen-day jail sentence. "Virus Squads" were dispatched to rooming houses, where police officers pinned down the homeless so that physicians could administer the vaccine. By the end of 1903, these highly questionable tactics helped to contain the epidemic.

In actual fact, Gallops Island was the site of a showdown between the board of health and one of the more vocal opponents of smallpox vaccinations. Dr. Immanuel Pfeiffer—who held that proper diet and cleanliness were the only reasonable means to ward off the disease—requested that he be allowed to visit the smallpox hospital on Gallops Island without the required vaccination. To silence critics, the chairman of Boston's board of health agreed. Two weeks after Pfeiffer's visit to the hospital

A Letter From
Sgt Warren E...
BOSTON, MASS
JUL 27
4-PM
1944

BUY U.S. SAVING
BONDS
ASK YOUR POSTM.

UNITED
STATES
POSTAGE

CENTS 3

Mr. + Mr. Joseph V. Field Jr.
88-60 Winchester Blvd
Bellerose, Long Island
New York

U. S. M. S.
RADIO TRAINING STATION
GALLUPS ISLAND
Boston, 10,   Massachusetts

on January 23, 1902, he was found critically ill in his Bedford home. "Sympathy for him is entirely lacking," reported *The Boston Globe*, "and the epithets applied to him are neither mild nor elegant, one of the least suggestive being that he is 'an old chump.'" Pfeiffer survived, and even though he remained stubbornly opposed to vaccination, his ordeal essentially put an end to the debate in Boston.

A little more than a decade later, the country was plunged into World War I. The ink had barely dried on the declaration of war against Germany, when on April 6, 1917, American sailors and Boston police boarded and seized German steamers that had found refuge in Boston Harbor when the war in Europe had begun. Nearly three hundred German officers and crew were taken as prisoners of war and imprisoned on Deer Island before being transferred to Gallops Island. Once on Gallops, they tended gardens, built houses, opened small workshops, and even laid out a tennis court.

When World War II broke out, Gallops Island again served in defense of the country. President Roosevelt realized that winning the war would require thousands of ships to carry supplies to the fronts, and the newly established U.S. Maritime Service was charged with training civilian volunteers to operate those vessels. From July 1940 to October 1945, the Radio Training Station on Gallops Island trained thousands of radio operators, with as many as fifty a week completing the twenty-week training program. Once graduated, these men became the ears of the ship. They were the first to hear warning signals of danger and responsible for tapping out the first calls for help.

The radio school was abandoned after the war. Foundations from some of the buildings remain along with broken concrete paths and the parade ground on the top of the island's drumlin. Ruins from the quarantine hospital also remain, along with fruit trees and flowering shrubs. Unfortunately, Gallops Island was closed in

2000 due to the presence of asbestos-containing debris among the ruins, and it's unclear when the island will reopen.

Perhaps, then, it's just as well that the monument to the Radio Training Station is no longer on the island's shores. While it may seem overshadowed in the North End park, a curious eye will appreciate this well-deserved tribute to the men who lost their lives in service to their country.

Platoon (March 1944) and letter home (upper left) courtesy of Don Wagner.

ADDITIONAL INFORMATION

A number of secure moorings are available through the Spectacle Island Marina. Call: 857-452-7221, or hail the Spectacle Island Marina on VHF 69. Reservations are advised.

Nixes Mate

Just north of Gallops Island lies a simple beacon with a peculiar name—Nixes Mate. The six-sided pyramid, familiar to some as the logo for the Friends of the Boston Harbor Islands, is perched on a mighty square base of granite blocks. The purpose of the black-and-white striped marker is to warn boaters of the dangerous gravel shoal on which it stands—but in a way, it's also a memorial to an island lost to the sea.

It's hard to believe looking at it today, but during the 1600s, Nixes Mate was a twelve-acre island in the heart of Boston Harbor. It was so large that it was used for pasturing sheep. By 1805, when the beacon was erected, all that remained were rocky flats covered at high tide. Where did the island go?

According to one salty yarn, centuries ago a Captain Nix was killed at sea and his mate was charged with the murder. Despite protesting his innocence, Nix's mate was sentenced to death and taken to the island to be hung. Before his execution, the accused prophesized that the island would be washed away by the angry sea as proof of his innocence. Still another legend has it that Nix was a pirate who sailed into Boston Harbor with a ship laden with treasure. After anchoring near the island, he and his mate went ashore and buried their booty. But according to this account, Captain Nix was unconvinced his mate could keep the secret, so Nix buried him along with the loot.

Not to spoil a good story, but considerably less-thrilling facts hold that over two hundred years of waves and wind have whittled the island away, as did the extraction of stone for ballast. And, given that the isle was referred to as Nixes Island as far back as 1636—six years after the Puritans arrived in Boston, when it was granted to John Gallop, the namesake of Gallops Island—the legends seem even more unlikely.

Nixes Mate still has a colorful history connected with pirates who lurked along the New England coast, pounced on their unsuspecting prey (even in sight of Outer Brewster Island), and threatened Boston's maritime commerce. In the 1700s, several convicted pirates were executed and then buried on Nixes Mate. One buccaneer met a more ignominious fate. William Fly was a pirate chief who led a mutiny aboard the slave ship *Elizabeth* in 1726, casting the captain and chief mate overboard. Following his capture, he was condemned to death along with two others. According to *The Boston News-Letter* account in its July 14, 1726, issue, "Their bodies were carried in a boat to a small island called Nick's Mate, about two leagues from the town, where Fly was hung up in irons, as a spectacle for the warning of others, especially sea-faring men." Fly's body hung on the gibbet chains on Nixes Mate like a scarecrow, his flesh plucked to pieces by sea birds until his bare bones rattled in the breeze. Bird Island, now buried somewhere under the runways at Logan Airport, was another harbor island where executed sea robbers were hung in chains as a gruesome warning to mariners considering hoisting the black flag.

While the golden age of piracy ended in the 1730s, they remained a curse as late as 1832, when Spanish pirates from the *Panda* boarded the *Mexican*, based in Salem, Massachusetts. The pirates robbed the *Panda* of $20,000 in silver and unsuccessfully attempted to kill the crew by setting fire to the vessel. They were eventually captured, brought to Boston, and sentenced to death. Captain Pedro Gilbert and four accomplices were hung in front of a crowd of more than 20,000 people on a spring morning in 1835. Apparently, one of the condemned attempted suicide the night before by inflicting a deep gash on the left side of his neck with a piece of tin. He never regained consciousness, but he was still taken to the gallows, seated in a chair, and executed when the trap door opened. The pirates proclaimed their innocence to the end, but—unlike the legendary mate of Captain Nix—they were kind enough not to consign any islands to the bottom of Boston Harbor.

Rainsford Island

Little clues to the past are scattered across Rainsford Island—reminders left behind by the people who shaped the rich history of this intriguing island. Like many of the islands in Boston Harbor, Rainsford housed the more "troublesome" members of Boston's population. For nearly two centuries, this small isle was home to a quarantine hospital, almshouse, veterans' house, and boys' reformatory. But Rainsford wasn't all gloom and doom—a thriving summer resort flourished there as well.

The incoming tide is known to dredge up fragments of these earlier days. For the keen observer, a walk along the beach could yield a pipe stem, a buffalo nickel, a piece of stoneware, or a belt buckle of a Civil War veteran. The most vivid reminders of the past, however, are found on the rocky outcrops on the south side of the island. There, previous islanders meticulously carved their inscriptions into the slate. Dr. Jerome Van Crowninshield Smith, who became mayor of Boston in 1854, left his mark: "J.V.C. Smith appointed Physician Of this Island 1826." Latin inscriptions, such as: "Es Deus quia vides omnia negotia —William Kendall, 1835," drive home the point that this isn't your typical graffiti. (Translation: You are God because you see all business.) One crudely drawn inscription on the rocks may also be the most curious: "1647." If that truly is the year it was made, it was done by one of the earliest European settlers—perhaps by Edward Rainsford himself, the colonist who settled on the island in 1636.

Rainsford, the first ruling elder of the Old South Church, received permission from John Winthrop to raise cattle on the island. Colonists used the island for farming and grazing until 1737, when Rainsford Island replaced Spectacle Island as the site of Boston's quarantine station. From then on the island was also somberly referred to as "Hospital Island" or "Pest House Island." Though unpleasant, the island served an important function. After the arrival of European settlers, typhoid, yellow fever, and smallpox were highly contagious and lethal diseases that constantly threatened Boston, and the Rainsford Island quarantine station provided a vulnerable population with a critical layer of protection.

Smallpox was a particularly virulent scourge on Boston, and epidemics in Boston were all-too-common occurrences well into the 1800s, with the last major epidemic occurring in Boston as late as 1903. One potent outbreak of the "speckled monster" coincided with the siege of Boston in 1775 and 1776. Indeed, smallpox may have played an even greater role in the American Revolution than it is typically given credit. George Washington—who was immune from smallpox as he'd survived the disease at the age of nineteen—suspected the British of bioterrorism. In a letter to the Continental Congress on December 4, 1775, he recounted testimony of a sailor claiming that the British had deliberately infected a number of people coming out of Boston "with [the] design of spreading the smallpox through this country and camp." Ten days later, after seeing an increasing number of cases in people leaving Boston, Washington reiterated his suspicion that smallpox was "a weapon of defense they are using against us." While it is impossible to know for certain if the British employed germ warfare, we do know that by 1776 there were more than five thousand reported cases of smallpox, making the patriots somewhat reluctant to return to the city after the British evacuation.

Smallpox epidemics persisted, fueled by the increase in immigration of the mid-1800s. Boats from the West Indies and Europe were the primary vessels carrying pestilence to the city. Physicians would inspect Boston-bound ships before docking at the wharves and quarantine sick passengers and crew. Sometimes boats would anchor off Rainsford Island for days before receiving an all-clear. (The *Beaver*, one of the three ships involved in the Boston Tea Party, spent a week off Rainsford in quarantine until it was released the night before the colonists dumped the tea in the harbor.)

A 1756 law spelled out the procedure for inbound ships: "Inquiry shall be made by the officer on duty at Castle William [Castle Island], of every vessel coming from the sea ... and if any vessel inquired of as aforesaid shall have any sickness on board, and upon further inquiry the same shall appear to be the plague, smallpox, or any other malignant infectious distemper, in such case shall be given to the master or commander of such vessel to anchor as near the hospital at Rainsford's Island as conveniently may be." Once cleared by the quarantine station at Rainsford, the master of the vessel had twenty-four hours to deliver certificates and flags declaring the vessel free from disease to the health office at Faneuil Hall.

In addition to those arriving by sea, infected Bostonians were sometimes transported to the isolated island. Some of those quarantined on Rainsford Island never left and were laid to rest on the west side of the island. It's been said that those who died of the disease in the city itself were occasionally buried on Rainsford, too. On such occasions, a city employee would row to the mainland under the cover of darkness, absconding back to the island with the potentially infectious body. Hundreds, if not thousands, of people were buried on Rainsford Island. In the 1930s, the bodies were reinterred on Long Island. However, since the workers lacked detailed maps of the burial ground, it's almost certain there are still remains on the island.

Rainsford Island continued to play a vital role in controlling the smallpox epidemics throughout the nineteenth century, and its limited resources were put to the test as the harbor's activity increased. By 1832, it was clear that the smallpox hospital facilities would need to be improved, and a magnificent three-story Greek Revival stone structure was built on a perch on the island's rocky southwest corner. The glorious Stone Hospital would have been a towering sight to those sailing into the harbor. Its soaring white columns, reminiscent of the Parthenon, earned it the nickname of the "Greek Temple."

Strangely enough, Rainsford Island hosted tourists at a summer resort between epidemics. It may not exactly have been Club Med, but the island provided plenty of amusement. The Old Mansion House on the island's eastern bluff was built in 1819, and provided summer accommodations in addition to quarters for the island keeper's and resident physician's families. Guests enjoyed the licensed tavern and reading room filled with all the principal newspapers from across the country. When there

were no infectious patients about, summer parties overflowed the hospital buildings with guests enjoying copious amounts of chowder and champagne.

City Archaeologist Ellen Berkland leads a group on a survey of Rainsford Island.

The quarantine station was moved to Deer Island in the 1840s, but Rainsford Island continued its institutional missions. It became the site of an almshouse in 1852, and, after the Civil War, a home to veterans of that awful conflict. In 1895, Rainsford Island hosted the House of Reformation, renamed the Suffolk School for Boys in the early twentieth century. Young men between the ages of eight and sixteen were kept busy in the island's print, shoe, and garment shops. One of the harbor's most interesting characters—Portuguese Joe—made his home just off the south coast of Rainsford Island, on what is known as Quarantine Rocks. Portuguese Joe was a lobsterman forced off Long Island in the 1890s. While other lobstermen floated their houses to Peddocks, Portuguese Joe decided to build on the exposed terrain off Rainsford's shore. He floated out the timber and used dry eelgrass under the floor boards and inside the walls as insulation. Somehow his house and shanties remained upright for forty-odd years. Everyone thought Joe was crazy, but Portuguese Joe's became

Rainsford's Island, Boston Harbor. *Photograph © the Museum of Fine Arts Boston. This 1840s oil painting by Robert Salmon depicts both the harbor activity and the Stone Hospital on Rainsford Island.*

ELLEN BERKLAND, CITY ARCHAEOLOGIST

The Boston Harbor Islands provide the most unspoiled archaeological sites in the city of Boston. Ellen Berkland explains the archaeological importance of the islands and what to do if you locate an artifact.

"The Boston Harbor Islands have not been impacted or developed to the same extent as the rest of the city, so the potential for finding ancient sites is extremely high. The islands offer us an amazing look at the peopling of New England and Boston over a span of eleven thousand years. Native Americans didn't leave any documents, so we're learning about their daily lives and activities through our findings on the islands. The shell middens provide a wonderful resource for recovering intact remains. There have been vibrant communities on the islands for thousands of years, and perhaps the most important part of our archaeological work is giving voice to the people who called them home.

The Boston Harbor Islands are part of an archaeological district, and its resources, both below ground and above ground, are protected under federal mandate. If you find an artifact, leave it as you found it for the next person to enjoy. If you believe you have found something significant, note the location, take a photograph, and call the state archaeologist at the Massachusetts Historical Commission. I always tell people to follow the mantra: Take nothing but pictures, and leave nothing but footprints."

a harbor landmark and a popular place to buy lobsters nonetheless.

The Suffolk School for Boys closed in 1920, and the city of Boston was unsuccessful in its attempt to sell the island. The city burned down the remaining buildings on the island in the 1930s, so little remains of these structures today. The ledge on the southwest part of Rainsford Island where the Greek Temple once surveyed the harbor is now a grassy area. The temple has been reduced to rubble.

Below that perch are the rocky outcrops where island occupants left their inscriptions. (Unfortunately, vandals have used less artistic graffiti to paint over some of these carvings.) In the opposite direction, toward the city skyline, is the site of the cemetery, now overgrown with tall grasses. There are no headstones, and save for a few bollards that presumably supported table-top tombs, no other evidence of the cemetery remains.

A robust lilac hedge, which harkens back to the nineteenth century when cultivated gardens dotted the landscape, separates the cemetery from the sandbar that connects the two drumlins of Rainsford Island. The isthmus provides a prime spot for kayakers and boaters to come ashore. (All that is left of the dock are the rotting posts on the island's south shore.)

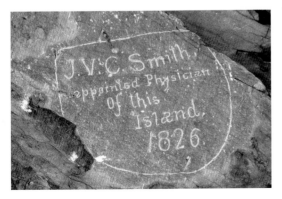

The eastern drumlin of Rainsford Island, while graded down, still provides the highest lookout on the island at nearly fifty feet. Rainsford does not have maintained hiking trails, so it's a bit of an effort to mount the hill through the brush. Remnants of the apple, plum, and peach orchards, however, do remain. The eastern end, atop an eroding bluff, provides great vistas of Georges and Peddocks Island. Watch your step for vestiges of the wells and foundations from institutional use of the island.

Rainsford Island is owned and maintained by the city of Boston and is its easternmost point. Camping is not allowed; and, unfortunately, vandals have desecrated some of the historical remnants. However, unvarnished reminders of the past remain on Rainsford Island, and it's a place that sets your imagination loose to ponder centuries of Boston history.

ADDITIONAL INFORMATION

Secure moorings are available through the Spectacle Island Marina. Call: 857-452-7221 or hail VHF 69. Reservations advised.

Moon Island

Sadly, Moon Island's story is not as pretty as its name.

For centuries, Boston's sewage was discharged into drains along the streets that emptied into the city's streams and bays. By the 1870s, this rudimentary system posed a considerable threat to public health, and a special commission recommended construction of a new system, which used intercepting sewers, tunnels, and pump stations to transport Boston's sewage to the gigantic reservoirs on Moon Island. The four granite lagoons, capable of holding fifty million gallons of raw sewage at a time, were released twice a day into Quincy Bay with the outgoing tides. This state-of-the-art treatment system was used into the 1970s, with engineers and scientists speculating that the harbor's currents would carry the sewage well away from the city, where it would be oxidized by the water or assimilated by sea animals. We all know how well that theory worked out.

Today, Moon Island is a stepping stone between Long Island and the Squantum section of Quincy, and it is a place where new classes of recruits take their first steps to becoming Boston firefighters. The Boston Fire Department's academy on the north side of Moon Island trains new recruits during fourteen-week sessions, and current firefighters receive ongoing education at the training center, which includes concrete structures used to simulate fire scenes. In addition, the Boston Police Department uses the island for a shooting range and disposal of suspected bombs and other explosives. Due to these uses, access to Moon Island is understandably restricted.

Thanks to ever-improving water quality in Boston Harbor, an increasing number of recreational divers are hunting for lobsters and exploring shipwrecks on the ocean floor. Victor Mastone, director of the Massachusetts Board of Underwater Archaeological Resources (BUAR), talks about what divers need to keep in mind while submerged.

"The Massachusetts Board of Underwater Archaeological Resources is the sole trustee of the Commonwealth's underwater heritage, promoting and protecting the public's interests in these resources. We encourage people to visit sites but not to disturb them. No one can damage, displace, or destroy an underwater resource without the board's permission. The exception is with exempt shipwrecks, which preserve such sites for the continued enjoyment of the recreational diving community.

"The outer harbor tends to attract more diving interest, but now that the harbor is clearing up, I think we'll see some activity coming back to the inner harbor. Most of the activity in the outer harbor is lobstering. There are a number of burned barges submerged in the general area of Calf Island that have a lot of structure, which the marine growth love and makes for very good lobstering."

EXEMPTED SHIPWRECKS

Currently, the BUAR lists three exempted sites in the Boston Harbor:

City of Salisbury: This steel freighter sank on April 22, 1938, bound for New York with a cargo valued at $2 million that included tropical animals. The *City of Salisbury*'s fate came at the long end of a troubled voyage: a Himalayan bear escaped while in Calcutta, a king cobra cannibalized its mate while at sea, and twenty-five monkeys jumped ship in Halifax. As Captain Lewis steered the ship toward the outer harbor a thick fog rolled in and the vessel impaled itself on uncharted rocks. Luckily, the pythons, cobras, monkeys, and rare birds were removed before the ship broke in two. Talk about invasive species!

Boston Harbor

Kiowa: The *Kiowa* was a steel freighter built in 1903 at Philadelphia and sank on December 26th of the same year. Due to blinding snow and poor visibility, Captain Chichester anchored the vessel near the approach of Nantasket Roads. The *Admiral Dewey*, another steamer bound for Jamaica, collided into the *Kiowa* as it was leaving Nantasket Roads. The force of the collision almost capsized the *Kiowa*, and the ship began to take on water fast. The *Cormorant*, an inbound tugboat, answered the *Kiowa*'s distress signals and Captain Chichester ordered his crew to jump for their lives. The U.S. Government eventually removed the wreck as it was an impediment to navigation. Today, most of the remaining debris is flat.

Romance: This steel-hulled passenger vessel sank just north of Graves Light in Broad Sound on September 9, 1936. *Romance* and its 208 passengers were returning from a day trip to Cape Cod when another steamer, the *New York*, emerged from an impenetrable fog, a scant six hundred feet from the *Romance*'s port beam. Attempts to avoid a collision were unsuccessful, and it became clear that the *Romance* would go down. Within fifteen minutes of the collision the *Romance* was already assuming its watery resting place—luckily, everyone aboard had been evacuated. Located within the Boston shipping channel, the *Romance* is considered "deep, dark, and dangerous." Charters who frequent this wreck typically require advanced certification.

77

Long Island

When Dennis Lehane conjured up the setting for his novel *Shutter Island*, which was made into a Hollywood thriller, he tapped into a childhood experience on Long Island when his uncle terrified him with creepy ghost tales about patients in the island's old hospital. While Shutter Island and its sprawling hospital for the criminally insane are fictitious, it mirrors the real-life history of the Boston Harbor Islands.

For centuries, Boston turned to its harbor islands to sequester and provide for those suffering from the physical and social ills that tend to fester in urban environments. While these social institutions have disappeared from the rest of the harbor islands, the tradition of providing vital human-service programs to those in need endures on Long Island.

In colonial times, due to the height of its three drumlins and its strategic location commanding the entrance to the inner harbor, Long Island played a key role in Boston's military history. In its darkest day, it was among the internment sites for Native Americans during King Philip's War. A century later, during the Revolutionary War, Long Island was a much-needed source of livestock and hay for the British holed up in Boston. On a July night in 1775, Continental soldiers snuck onto the island, stole the cattle and sheep, and took seventeen Loyalist prisoners. The patriots even launched a daring daylight raid the next morning to burn the remaining farm buildings and seventy tons of bundled hay that was about to be shipped to the British in Boston.

Left: Today, the Public Health Commission's Long Island campus continues the proud tradition of assisting those in need.

Latitude: 42° 19' 48.22" North
Longitude: 70° 57' 25.58" West

After the British fled Boston in March 1776, Washington's army occupied Long Island and built defensive batteries on its northern bluff. In June 1776, a fierce battle erupted as the troops fired on a British transport ship carrying Scottish reinforcements—apparently, the Scots hadn't been informed that their fellow soldiers had already skipped town. Approximately forty Scottish soldiers were killed, and it's possible they were buried somewhere on the island.

During the Civil War, soldiers traveling to and from the battlefields of the South drilled and trained at Long Island's Camp Wightman. The camp was later renamed Fort Strong in honor of a Civil War general. During both World Wars, enlisted men at the fort were responsible for laying and controlling mines in the northern channel of Boston Harbor. Even after the fort was deserted at the conclusion of World War II, Long Island housed two Nike missile batteries in the 1950s. (The city used one of the abandoned missile base buildings in the 1970s to store surplus books from the Boston Public Library.)

Crumbling bunkers and concrete gun emplacements from Fort Strong still occupy Long Island Head, the drumlin on the northeastern tip of the island. Near those ruins, barely peering above the ever-growing tree line, is Long Island Head Light. The current white brick lighthouse, dating from 1901, rises fifty-two feet in height and is the fourth beacon to grace the island's northern bluff.

At the base of Long Island Head is Camp Harbor View, the newest addition to Long Island. This co-ed camp was designed to help alleviate the growing trend of violence among Boston teenagers, which can be particularly acute during summer months. Opened in 2007, the camp hosts hundreds of inner-city children from Boston neighborhoods. For many children, the camp is their first introduction to the harbor.

This is not the first summer camp on Long Island, however. At the turn of the twentieth century, the Municipal Camp for Boys hosted as many as a thousand campers each summer for week-long programs focused on recreation and discipline. Unlike

Camp Harbor View on Long Island is dedicated to serving the needs of inner-city children.

Camp Harbor View, boys wore uniforms, camped in tents, and rose to a reveille at six o'clock each morning. The present-day incarnation is a far kinder, gentler place, providing boys and girls ages eleven to fourteen with the true summer experience every child deserves.

To the south of Camp Harbor View is the institutional campus maintained by the Boston Public Health Commission. In the 1880s, after failed attempts to develop the island as a resort, the city purchased most of the island to host Boston's charitable institutions. A hotel, built in the 1840s, was converted into an almshouse for the indigent, and a chronic disease hospital; a nursing school and a home for unwed mothers were added later. To make room for these new residents, the city forcibly removed a small village of Portuguese fishermen living on the east side of the island in 1887. Many of the Portuguese fishermen floated their shacks across the harbor and settled on Peddocks Island, creating the cottage colony that still endures.

Today, the Long Island campus provides health services and shelter, as well as a variety of vital programs to transition people beyond homelessness. One of the most innovative programs might be The Serving Ourselves Farm, which grows fresh produce for use in the shelters, while providing work opportunities for homeless men and women.

While Long Island has a number of historical sights and great potential as a recreation area, public access is understandably restricted because of its institutional use.

ADDITIONAL INFORMATION

A number of secure moorings are available through the Spectacle Island Marina. Call: 857-452-7221, or hail the Spectacle Island Marina on VHF 69. Reservations are advised.

For more information about Camp Harbor View:
www.campharborviewfoundation.org

Is There Buried Treasure in Boston Harbor?

Sure, pirates lurked in the waters of the Caribbean, but like many of today's vacationers, bygone buccaneers enjoyed summer in New England, too. During the 1600s and 1700s, sea bandits such as Blackbeard and William Kidd preyed on many ships sailing in and out of Boston.

Treasure hunters have long been fueled by rumors that pirates buried their booty or hid their ill-gotten goods amid the islands of Boston Harbor. If they did, they unfortunately took the whereabouts to their graves. Still, tales surrounding the lost treasure of the infamous Captain Kidd, arrested in Boston in 1699 before being shipped to London for execution, persist. A letter from Kidd, which turned out to be a forgery, claimed he buried two treasure chests on Conant's Island, now part of Logan Airport. Other stories claim that Kidd hid silver and gold on the coast of Winthrop near Deer Island. Likewise, the pirate "Long Ben" Avery was said to have buried a stash of diamonds on Gallops Island—which, curiously, have yet to be found.

But it's not just pirate tales luring those in search of buried treasure. Hundreds of ships have met an untimely demise

among the islands, scattering their contents on the island shores or taking their cargoes to the bottom of the sea. The most notorious wreck was that of the 74-gun French man-of-war *Magnifique*, which was said to have carried gold and silver when it sank off Lovells Island in 1782. Despite evidence that the French crew offloaded its valuable cargo, dreams of finding silver and gold coins still pique the interest of treasure hunters.

So, is there really treasure buried on the islands of Boston Harbor? Aargh! If we knew for sure, do you think we'd tell you?

From top: Blackbeard, Captain Kidd (executed in London, strung up in gibbets), and "Long Ben" Avery

81

Boston

Light *Swim*

One August day in 1910, little Rose Pitonof swam through Boston Harbor, head bobbing up and down in the surf with every breaststroke. Rose was on her way to the record books and international fame by becoming the first woman—and only the second person—to swim the nearly ten-mile distance from the pier of Charlestown Bridge to Boston Light on Little Brewster Island. (Alois

peted the accomplishment of the "stocky little phenomenon of the water." News of Rose's feat quickly spread around the world. Suddenly propelled into fame, Rose spent the next six years headlining a renowned vaudeville circuit, performing diving and swimming feats in a water tank before sell-out audiences across the country. She continued to set long-distance swimming records in

Boston Light Swim. Conditions can be grueling. These marathon swimmers battle powerful cross-currents, boat traffic, and strong gusts of wind. But it's the frigid water, even in August, that can pose the greatest challenge. "As soon as you jump into the harbor, you feel the air rush out of your lungs," says Kornbau.

Anderle had been the first person to complete the swim, but his result was disputed because he crawled over the bar at Nixes Mate during low tide.) Battling cold water, cross-currents, winds, and waves, Rose completed the swim in six hours and fifty minutes. Seven men tried to make the journey that day. All gave up. What made Rose's amazing feat all the more remarkable was that she was only fifteen years old.

Banner headlines on the front page of *The Boston Daily Globe* trum-

Boston, New York City, and London.

Today, long-distance swimmers such as Elaine Kornbau carry on the proud tradition of traversing the harbor in the annual Boston Light Swim. Held every August, the 8-mile swim from Boston Light to the L Street Bathhouse in South Boston is called the "granddaddy of American open-water marathons." The race draws elite open-water swimmers from countries as far away as Egypt.

There's nothing "light" about the effort required to complete the

Depending on conditions, most swimmers take between three and six hours to complete the course, although the record is under two-and-a-half hours. For swimmers like Kornbau, the achievement is awe-inspiring. "Approaching the city skyline from the water is powerful; here I am swimming toward one of the world's most important cities, seeing it from an angle that few other people experience."

Those who prefer to stay dry can participate in the Boston Light Swim by serving on support boats that offer food, drink, and lots of encouragement to the swimmers. But whether you're manning the boat or bobbing along, there's no question about it—you're immersing yourself in history.

For more information:
www.bostonlightswim.org.

Thompson Island

Despite the fact that it is only a twenty-minute boat ride away, Thompson Island exudes the feeling of the deep wilderness. The rustling of birds and animals can be as startling as the wind blowing through the trees, and hours can pass without seeing another person—though abandoned campsites may have you wondering if you truly are alone. This eerie sensation is heightened when the path in front of you suddenly opens onto a clearing filled with startling structures reminiscent of military training grounds. Towering, wooden climbing walls supported by long wires soar above the tree line; tires and ropes hang from large wooden poles fastened together like a frame for a teepee. And a colossal web of rope looks as if Spiderman himself had recently visited. Just when you're ready to panic, the Boston skyline comes into view, and with it, the comforting reminder that civilization is within easy reach of this verdant sanctuary.

Henry Adams sardonically wrote of his hometown that "Boston is a curious place. Its business in life is to breed and to educate." Well, for nearly two hundred years Thompson Island has been fulfilling that latter civic obligation. Today, the Thompson Island Outward Bound Education Center proudly continues the tradition of using the island in educational service.

Long before its ultimate purpose was divined, however, Thompson Island was a hunting and fishing ground for Native Americans. An exploratory band of ten Pilgrims, in a quest to contact and trade with the Massachusett tribe, was among the first Europeans to set foot on the island's shores in 1621. Led by Miles Standish and with Squanto as a guide, it took almost a full day for the Pilgrims to reach Boston Harbor from Plymouth in their tiny shallop; but when they finally arrived, they were awed by the island-dotted harbor. "Better harbours for shipping cannot be than here are," they reported. So impressed were the Pilgrims that they regretted the hand of God had not guided them to Boston Harbor as their final destination in the New World. William Bradford, Governor of Plymouth Colony, wrote that the expedition "brought home a good quantity of beaver, and made report of the place, wishing they had been there settled (but it seems the Lord, who assigns to all men the bounds of their habitations, had appointed it for another use)."

Standish and the Pilgrims claimed the island for a Scot, David Thompson, who was the acting governor of New England and said to be the first European settler in New Hampshire. In 1626, Thompson established a trading post on the island to swap beaver furs and fish with the Native Americans. His cabin on the eastern side of the island may have been the first permanent colonial structure in Boston.

The island was granted to Dorchester in 1634, and the town voted in 1639 to rent it to property holders for twenty pounds a year. The income afforded the town a schoolmaster, who taught writing, English, Latin, and other languages to main-land children, beginning the island's long-running connection with educating the city's youth.

It wasn't until nearly two centuries later, however, that Thompson Island's educational mission was formally realized. A group of Boston philanthropists, concerned about the welfare of boys in the city, purchased the island and established the Boston Farm School to teach them agricultural and vocational skills.

It is believed that Charles Bulfinch—the famed architect who gave Boston the golden dome of the State House—designed the great brick Greek Revival building perched on the island's summit that housed most of the school's students and faculty. The inaugural class of fourteen boys arrived on Thompson Island in 1833, and an educational institution of one sort or another has remained there ever since.

Soon after it opened, the Farm School merged with the Boston Asylum for Indigent Boys, which was founded in the wake of the War of 1812 to care for boys left orphaned and destitute by the fighting. Students divided their time between farm work, study, and play. They also performed domestic duties such as cooking, baking, and laundry. Students planted oak, maple, and many other trees along with pear and apple orchards, many of which remain today. These Farm School vestiges make Thompson Island one of the few places on the harbor islands where mature woodlands are found.

City Hall on Cottage Row.
Courtesy Archives and Special Collections
Department, Healey Library, University of
Massachusetts, Boston. Thompson Island Collection.

The school was granted legal guardianship of the boys until they reached the age of twenty-one. Even though many students were in clear sight of home, they could only return to visit during two weeks in the summer. Nathaniel Hawthorne, who visited the island in 1837, noted how detached the boys were from the constant activity of Boston and its busy harbor. "The farm boys remain insulated," he wrote, "looking at the passing show, within sight of the city, yet having nothing to do with it; beholding their fellow-creatures skimming by them in winged machines, and steamboats snorting and puffing through the waves. Methinks an island would be the most desirable of all landed property, for it seems like a little world by itself."

One of its claims to fame is that the Farm School was home to the first school band in the U.S. In 1857, Headmaster William Morse overheard a group of students entertaining themselves with a makeshift "orchestra," outfitted with instruments made from combs covered by tissue paper. Seizing upon their initiative, Morse bought his students brass instruments, and the band was formed. Six school alumni would go on to become members of the Boston Symphony Orchestra.

The school also provided a unique model community, dubbed Cottage Row—and if Hawthorne thought the school was a little world unto itself in 1837, he should have seen Cottage Row, nearly fifty years later. Cottage Row began in the summer of 1888 when some of the boys erected a row of tents on the north end of the island in which they lived. The next year, using skills they'd learned from their manual training, the boys erected twelve wooden cottages. Possession of these small, one-room cottages dotting the shoreline was divided into shares transferable through the school bank.

Cottage Row became a mock city that served as a practical civics lesson for the boys. The cabins included a city hall and a library of thee hundred volumes. The boys elected a mayor, assessor, clerk, police, street commissioner, and jury members. An appointed judge oversaw judicial proceedings, and justice could be severe. A group of boys arrested for playing marbles on Sunday faced fines of up to thirty-five cents; another boy convicted of annoying the goat was condemned to feed and water "Nannie" for a month.

In the 1900s, the school became known as the Farm and Trade School. Students from ten to fourteen years of age split their time between studying and learning an industrial trade or occupation, such as carpentry, cabinetry, woodworking, mechanical drawing, blacksmithing, and printing. The school's print shop even provided Boston hotels with their handbills, and three upper grades had practical study in meteorology.

Over the years, a variety of interesting—and strange—proposals have been floated for Thompson Island. For example, in the 1990s the city of Boston proposed using the island as a training camp for the New England Patriots football team. But the most grandiose plan called for the island to be part of a site for a huge international exposition in 1976 to celebrate the American bicentennial. The planners of Expo '76 projected that up to sixty million people would visit the 690-acre fairground, which, in addition to Thompson Island, would have been located on Columbia Point in Dorchester and a new harbor island created from a combination of landfill and floating platforms.

The plan called for construction of a 500-boat marina and a hotel on the southern end of Thompson Island as well as the conversion of the school facilities into a youth camp and demonstration farm. Visitors would have been able to rent bikes or electric cars to traverse the island. And if the concept of electric cars back in the 1970s wasn't weird enough, the exposition planners wanted to build a huge, transparent dome that would cover part of the island's natural landscape of grassy knolls, woods, and winding trails. This climate-controlled dome, more than two football fields in diameter, would ensure that boating, swimming, and picnicking could be enjoyed year round—even in the throes of a New England winter. Somehow these elaborate plans never came to fruition, and the island remains true to its educational legacy.

Since 1988, the island has been owned by the Thompson Island Outward Bound Education Center, making it the only Boston Harbor Island to be privately owned. Although it works with youth from all economic backgrounds and adults as well, its primary mission is to serve underprivileged Boston children by offering programs that instill teamwork, compassion, and self-confidence through experiential learning. Thompson Island Outward Bound serves more than five thousand students and adults each year. Students camp, scale those towering climbing walls, traverse that wily ropes course, and engage in mock search-and-rescue activities on and off the island. Corporations and youth group programs also use the Outward Bound facilities on Thompson Island for team-building retreats.

Given the vast amount of programming offered, Thompson Island is only open to public exploration on Sundays from June until Labor Day, but clearing a Sunday to make the trip is worth it. As one of the largest islands in the harbor, it's easy to spend an entire afternoon hiking through its 204 acres of varied landscapes.

Ferries leave from the EDIC dock at the Marine Industrial Park in South Boston, delivering you to the island in twenty minutes. Nearest the dock on Thompson Island are administrative buildings along with a library, a cafeteria, an auditorium, and a gymnasium. The quad of brick dormitories on the top of the hill will remind you of a leafy, Ivy League campus. There is also a conference center that hosts meetings, catered events, and even weddings—so if you're looking for a truly unique venue for your nuptials, consider tying the knot after completing the ropes course.

Away from the campus, dirt trails crisscross the island's deep woods and rolling meadows. One of the highlights is the salt marsh on the southern side. The marsh, with its rivulets and tall grasses, serves as a nursery for fish and shellfish. It is a popular stop-over for migrating shore birds in the spring and fall. In the summer, herons, egrets, and kill-deers can be found nesting in trees. In the spring and fall, migrating birds such as yellowlegs, geese, sandpipers, and teals can be spotted. In the winter, buffleheads and mergansers take up residence in the marsh.

The southern end of Thompson Island contains one of the most poignant plots of land on the Boston Harbor Islands. It is a graveyard dedicated to Farm School students who drowned in two of the most tragic events in the harbor's long history. In April 1842, as a reward for good behavior, a large group of students was treated to a fishing trip on the harbor. In sight of the Thompson Island shore and some of the other boys who attended the school, the *Polka*, the school's sloop, suddenly overturned and sank. Twenty-three boys, a teacher, and a boatman all drowned. Only four boys survived. *The Boston Daily Globe* reported of the incident: "It is one of those events of an inscrutable Providence, which occurring suddenly to so many youthful spirits, in the moment of joyous exhilaration and sending sorrow and mourning into so many families, cannot but excite in the breast of everyone a sympathy for the bereaved families, and a lively sense of the frail tenure of human existence."

Fifty years later, tragedy unfortunately struck again as another school sloop capsized between Spectacle Island and Thompson Island in a sudden squall. Ten students and an instructor were thrown into the frigid harbor and clung to the overturned craft, praying for a rescue that never came. The chill of the water and exhaustion were too much as they fell one by one into the sea. Four hours after it overturned, the boat drifted ashore with just two survivors still clutching the hull.

The graveyard is relatively untended. Native American remains discovered at a burial site on the northern end of the island were reinterred here, but the headstones were removed due to vandalism. It is believed these markers were stored and subsequently lost in a 1971 fire that destroyed the original Farm School building. A wooden kneeler with chipped and faded blue paint sits in front of the graveyard. A small sign reads:

The Thompson Island Outward Bound Educational Center provides "adventurous and challenging experiential learning programs that inspire character development, compassion, community service, environmental responsibility, and academic achievement." Arthur Pearson, president of the nonprofit organization, explains how the island location helps it to fulfill its mission.

"The physical attribute of having an island is that it — and any island — has its own charisma and allure by the nature of being separate and apart. Each one has its own character and personality. And by providing a vest pocket wilderness, Thompson Island allows us to do very powerful outdoor programming very close to home. For many kids in metropolitan Boston, it's their first time in the harbor or on a boat of that size, and stepping on the island's shore, they are as far from home as they have ever been, at least mentally and spiritually. Just that physical attribute of being a refuge is very powerful. We have the best of both worlds. We are right in the heart of the city with the ability to really feel and be in a wilderness environment.

"Some of the most magical places with students young and old are the climbing towers and ropes course. In some ways, it's the great equalizer. It's as important for the corporate chieftain as it is a fourteen-year-old starting something new and a lot of remarkable growth happens out there for children of all ages. The places many of our students also find to have a powerful impact on them, though in a much quieter way, are the salt marshes and shorelines where one can really capture a sense of the tranquility that Mother Nature offers when you are able to stop and listen."

"May the water and winds bless their souls, may their souls bless our hearts and our island."

Near the cemetery on the island's southern tip is a massive sand spit, exposed at low tide, that reaches nearly to Squantum on the mainland in Quincy. The mudflats in this area were a popular clamming spot for centuries. On the western side, a curved beach provides views across Dorchester Bay to the John F. Kennedy Library and the National Grid gas tank, that colorful landmark familiar to everyone who's sat in traffic on the Southeast Expressway. The beach becomes more sandy on the eastern shore of the island, facing Spectacle Island.

A small salt marsh on the easterly shore has been restored to allow tidal flow to resume. Now that tidal flushing has been reestablished, native salt marsh grasses and migrating shorebirds are returning to this side of Thompson Island. The marsh provides a nursery for fish such as striped bass and winter flounder.

Schools of fish will feel right at home on an island with such a rich history of education. And this small piece of wilderness in Boston's backyard continues to deliver lessons. By calling to the adventurer in each of us, Thompson Island teaches us about ourselves, our community, and our environment.

ADDITIONAL INFORMATION

⛔ Thompson Island is only open to public exploration on Sundays from June until Labor Day.

🪔 The MV Outward Bound ferry dock is located on Drydock Avenue near the Black Falcon Cruise Terminal and the Boston Design Center in the Marine Industrial Park, South Boston. The island encourages visitors to arrive early. There is a public parking lot about .25 miles down Drydock Avenue on the left. For more information and ferry schedules visit, www.thompsonisland.org.

 Rangers offer walking tours of Thompson Island's salt marshes and natural landscape on summer Sundays.

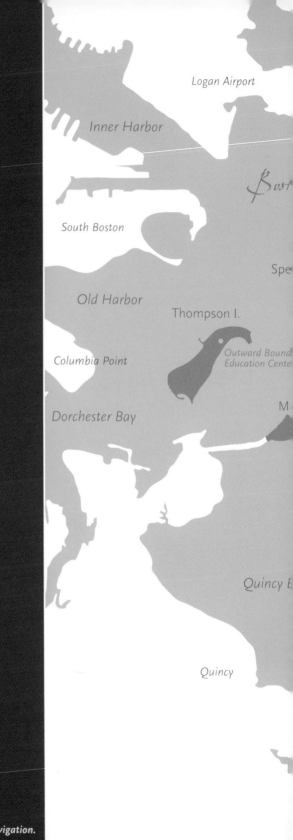

Logan Airport

Inner Harbor

Bost

South Boston

Spe

Old Harbor

Thompson I.

Columbia Point

Outward Bound
Education Cente

Dorchester Bay

M

Quincy B

Quincy

Map not intended for navigation.

Massachusetts Bay

The C

Gr

I.

Wastewater
Treatment
Plant

Deer I.

Green I.

Little Calf I.

Calf I.

Outer B

le Brewster I.

arbor

Long Island
Head

Nixes Mate

AROUND HINGHAM BAY

Shag Roc

Boston
Light

Long I.

Fort
Strong

Gallops I.

Fort Warren
Georges I.

Little Brewster I.

Rainsford I.

Fort
Andrews

Peddocks I.

Spinnaker I.

Hangman I.

Hingham Bay

Hull

Nut I.

Sheep I.

Bumpkin I.

Grape I.

Slate I.

World's End

Raccoon I.

Webb Memorial
Park

Langlee I.

Ragged I.

Sarah I.

_Hingham
Harbor_

Button I.

Weymouth

Hingham

Peddocks Island

The Boston Harbor Islands are filled with ruins of forts, hospitals, and other buildings that remind us of their rich collective history, and these shadowy remnants give us great insights into the city's unique heritage. But for centuries, the islands have also been called "home" by those who lived on their shores, providing countless personal, intimate memories of island life that the skeletons of old buildings simply can't begin to share.

Courtesy Claire Hale.

Today, the collection of nearly fifty summer cottages on Peddocks Island is the only community that remains on the Boston Harbor Islands. It's the last breathing connection to generations past, and these stalwart islanders endow Peddocks Island with a unique and wonderful character.

While some cottages have been abandoned and fallen into severe disrepair, others are quaint, well-kept clapboard homes adorned with lobster traps and buoys, painted in a bright rainbow of color. The history of the island is as colorful as the cottage paint jobs. The antecedents of some cottages date to 1887, when Portuguese fishermen and lobstermen floated (yes, floated) their families and houses over the open harbor to Peddocks Island after being forced to move from Long Island. There are captivating stories of bootleggers and gamblers in addition to childhood memories of carefree summer days that have spanned as many as five or six generations back to the original Portuguese lobstermen. This living history may not have much life left in it, however. Under an agreement with the state, the current islanders are slated to be the last of those allowed to live on Peddocks Island.

Islanders like to say Peddocks Island, located just a quarter mile from the Nantasket Peninsula across Hull Gut, is actually five islands in one because of its composition of five drumlins connected by sandy, gravel bars called "tombolos." The double drumlins of East Head contain the ruins of Fort Andrews; Middle Head is home to the summer cottages; while West Head and Princes Head offer nearly pristine environments. Since Peddocks Island is one of the harbor's largest and has the longest shoreline, it's easy to spend hours wandering the rocky beaches and exploring its varying topography, perhaps the most diverse of all the harbor islands. The trails on Peddocks Island take you past woodlands, scrubby sandbars, rocky beaches, brackish ponds, and salt marshes.

The island gained its name after English planter Leonard Peddock in the early 1600s, though there is evidence that Peddocks Island has been inhabited for thousands of years. One day in the 1960s, summer resident Josephine Walsh was shocked to discover a skeleton near her cottage on an eroded bluff of West Head. Carbon

Of the hundreds built according to a military template during World War II, it is believed that the Peddocks Island chapel is the only one of its design still standing.

Putting up the windmill for limited electricity was one of the chores when summer residents arrived to the island. Claire Hale's father, Victor Pierimarchi (above), and her uncle, Edigio Pierimarchi, in 1946. Courtesy Claire Hale.

dating determined the bones to be 4,100 years old, making it the oldest skeleton ever found in New England.

Europeans started farming the island as early as 1634, and the agricultural uses of Peddocks continued well into the American Revolution. Peddocks, not unlike other harbor islands, was one more site on which the day-to-day struggles of the American Revolution were played out. Both the patriots and British often turned to the island farms to seize supplies for their armies, or simply strip their foes of much-needed provisions. Indeed, in 1775, just a few months into the Revolutionary War, patriots raided a Loyalist farm on Peddocks Island and seized four hundred sheep and thirty head of cattle. The following year, six hundred patriot militiamen were stationed on the island to discourage the evacuated British from returning to the city.

Peddocks Island's destiny as a military site didn't end there. With the construction of Fort Andrews in 1898 at the onset of the Spanish-American War, the island played a role in protecting the city of Boston. The fort was built on eighty-eight acres donated by Eliza Andrews, widow of a former governor of Massachusetts, and named in honor of her uncle, Civil War general Leonard Andrews. Opened in 1904, Fort

Andrews housed artillery, gun batteries, and observation stations and was used heavily during World War I, preparing soldiers before their deployment to Europe. It was decommissioned after the war but reactivated with the onset of World War II.

One of the most noteworthy episodes in Fort Andrews' history may also be its most charming. During the latter half of World War II, more than one thousand Italian prisoners of war captured in North Africa were detained in the fort. The prisoners were originally held on Deer Island and in Camp McKay in South Boston, but after the fall of Mussolini and the surrender of Italy in 1943, the prisoners—no longer considered a threat—were moved to Fort Andrews and given considerable liberties. Peddocks Island was certainly no German stalag. In fact, American veterans were known to complain about the "pampering" of the former enemy forces. (Sixty years later, the benign conditions under which the Italian POWs lived would be cited in legal proceedings brought by foreign prisoners held at Guantanamo Bay, disgruntled about their treatment.) During the week, the Italian POWs worked at the Charlestown Navy Yard loading munitions on U.S. ships bound for the European theater of war. When

they weren't working, the Italian soldiers were relatively free to move about the fort and the island. They were given passes to visit Boston in groups of ten to twenty-five, provided they were chaperoned by an Army sergeant, and they could even receive visitors on weekends.

Italian-American families living on Peddocks Island and around Boston befriended many of the prisoners, some of whom lived in the same towns in Italy from

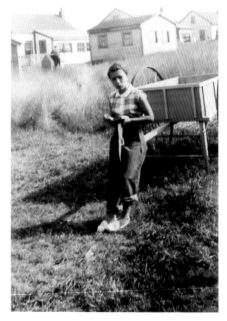

During World War II, Boston Harbor was closed because of mines. Summer residents to Peddocks took the Army boat and used carts such as these to transport their goods from the fort to the cottages. Courtesy Claire Hale.

The shuttered ruins of Fort Andrews appear spooky and magical all at once.

which the American families had emigrated. It wasn't uncommon to see the prisoners in the North End on Sundays. The prisoners spent the day going to mass and eating a home-cooked meal with sponsor families before taking the ferry back to the island. Italian-American women brought the prisoners food and supplies, and in some cases they fell in love and married. There were approximately fifty marriages between POWs and daughters or relatives of sponsor families.

At the conclusion of World War II, the Italians who hadn't married a Bostonian were sent back to their homeland, and the fort was abandoned. The East Head of the island, which was once completely barren, is now abundant with trees. Park management is working to make the fort ruins safe for visitors by stabilizing and restoring its dilapidated brick buildings and demolishing the ones that are beyond repair. The rusty fence that separated Fort Andrews from the civilian side of the island still stands, and a small stone marker imprinted with "US" is implanted in the beach on the island's west side.

On the outskirts of the fort, next to the dock, is a small, white chapel that served the fort and island residents. From a distance, the wooden chapel looks as if it was transplanted from the rolling hills of Vermont, though it's evident that it hasn't been used for years. The provenance of the chapel is quite interesting, however. It was one of hundreds built according to a military template used during World War II and believed to be the only one of its design still standing.

Within the boundaries of the fort on East Head, the asphalt roads remain. Once outside the fort, however, they become unpaved trails, with a single path leading from the dock all the way to the other end of the island at West Head. After leaving East Head, the trail traverses a tombolo flanked by rocky beaches and placid coves. Reaching Middle Head, the topography changes again; the trees return and the land rises once more.

Near the spot where the trail ascends Middle Head is the former site of the Island Inn, which was a popular destination for summer outings and boating parties in the early 1900s. The hotel was owned and operated by John Irwin, a former professional baseball player in the 1880s and 1890s. In the first decade of the twentieth century, Irwin helped organize "Ye Olde-Timers' Gambol," an annual reunion of retired ballplayers from as far back as the 1860s that drew upwards of two thousand players and fans. (One of the big stars was Arthur Cummings, considered the inventor of the curve ball.) The highlight of the day was a baseball game with the retired players in what may have been the first old-timers game ever organized in the United States.

Drunken parties, brawls, gambling, and prostitution all helped the Island Inn to earn its notorious reputation as the "Headache House Hotel." In 1909, following a "Chinese picnic," a euphemistic term for an opium party, Hull police arrested Irwin on charges of maintenance of a nuisance, illegal gaming, and illegally selling intoxicating liquors. William Drake, proprietor of the nearby West Head House and a former policeman, was also arrested and similarly charged. The complaints were filed by representatives of the Watch and Ward Society, whose censorship of books and performing arts was the origin of the phrase "Banned in Boston." Both men were found guilty and had to pay a small fine.

Drake's hotel burned down in 1913, and Irwin's hotel was gone a few years later. A small blue cottage on the eastern shore, which was at one time adjacent to the main lodge, is all that remains from the wild days of the Island Inn. A gazebo in front sold ice cream, but the cottage was the scene of the inn's more nefarious activities. On one side of the cottage was a bar and café, while the rooms on the other side were where ladies of the night plied their trade.

It may not be quite as lively, but the cottage colony on Middle Head has a colorful history as well. When the government purchased the land on East Head for the construction of Fort Andrews, the Portuguese fishermen and lobstermen who had relocated there from Long Island once again floated their shacks, this time to Middle Head. During Prohibition, the community had a flourishing bootlegging business, and rumrunners were known to hide their cargo in the island's coves. (And soldiers in search of a lobster dinner and some hooch were known to visit the island's civilian side.)

Summer residents joined the Portuguese lobstermen on Peddocks Island, drawn by its pure air,

The Living History of Peddocks Island

Claire and Bill Hale are among the last cottagers on Peddocks Island. Claire has spent her summers on the island for more than seventy years. She and Bill live in a two-story cottage on the former site of John Irwin's Island Inn. The cottage has been in Claire's family since 1948.

"My family has been coming here since 1917. My uncle did business with the Portuguese fishermen. When my uncle told them his son had rickets, they told him to come to Peddocks Island and put him out in the sun for the summer. So he rented a cottage and stayed all summer. And when he took the boy back to the doctor in the fall, his legs had straightened out. So my uncle bought a cottage.

"When my father came to this country from Italy he was eleven years old. Peddocks Island was the first place his older brother took him. And when my father met my mother, he took her here and she fell in love. My father came here until he was seventy-five years old. At one point our family had ten cottages on Peddocks. We turned the island from Portuguese to half-Italian!

"During the war, the Italian prisoners started coming to the cottages on Sunday when they didn't have to work. They had a grand old time. I remember all these soldiers with 'Italy' written on their uniforms. Just before they were sent back, my grandmother had them visit our house in Somerville. Our house was surrounded by MPs with guns. We were the only Italians on the street in a mostly Irish neighborhood, so you can imagine all the neighbors were on their porches.

"When I was a teenager, we would go to Princes Head every single night and have a bonfire. We sang 'Goodnight Irene' at the end of the bonfire. Without the cottages, Peddocks is going to lose history that started with the Portuguese fishermen from the Azores who came here to help the fishing industry in Boston. It will be a shame."

The Italian POWs commemorating their visit to Argentina and Giuseppe Bassignana's home in Somerville. The prisoners were shipped back to Italy shortly thereafter. Courtesy Claire Hale.

Claire Hale's family. (Claire is the little girl seated in the first row.) Water from the well was poured into the tank on the left for running water inside the cottage. Courtesy Claire Hale.

cool nights, and lulling waves. At its peak, the cottage village had hundreds of residents during the summer months. A general store sold goods to residents, and the Tea Room sold penny candy and ice cream. Middle Head even had its own unofficial "mayor," Mabel Pinto.

Today, the scene on Middle Head is quite different. There are far fewer residents, occupying a hodgepodge of quaint cottages and ramshackle shacks. (There are a handful of year-round residents on Peddocks Island, too.) There is no electricity or running water since the power and water lines were severed. Residents rely on generators, propane, oil lanterns, car batteries, and solar panels for power and light. Rainwater is collected in plastic rain barrels, and some cottages have well water.

Even more difficult for long-time islanders, some of whom still summer on the island from Vermont and Florida, is the sense that they've become *persona non grata* in the eyes of the state, which took ownership of Peddocks Island in 1970. The state has sought to evict the islanders, arguing that the cottages are private use of public land and a source of pollution. A compromise reached in 1992 allows the present residents to remain until their deaths. At that point, the cottages will pass into the ownership of the state. Currently, cottagers pay an annual permit fee to the state, which owns the land but not the structures. Since the compromise was reached, residents have passed away or given up their homes, and no more than thirty cottages are currently inhabited.

The West Head of Peddocks Island offers a sharp contrast to the summer colony of Middle Head, as it is largely uninhabited. At a pink cottage on Middle Head, the main path across the island veers to the left and traverses another sandy tombolo.

Once on West Head, this grassy pathway leads through dense foliage, enveloping you in a breathtaking tunnel of green. The path ends at a narrow, rocky beach with a view directly across the water to Nut Island. During World War II, for fear of German U-boats wandering into the Boston Harbor, submarine nets were erected between the West Head and Nut Island (and across Hull Gut from Fort Andrews to Hull, too).

The elevated, eroding bluff of Princes Head juts off from the east side of Peddocks Island, and is where soldiers at Fort Andrews practiced military maneuvers. In the 1870s, the bluff was the target for cannon tests taking place at Nut Island (see page 206). To walk out to Princes Head, approach it from the north, along the beach near Middle Head.

Despite being barren as recently as sixty years ago, Peddocks Island has evolved into a vibrant ecosystem. The ruins of Fort Andrews are surrounded by a dense woodland of mature and sapling pine, maple, birch, apple, and cottonwood trees, which attract owls and hawks. Apple and pear trees from the Army orchard remain. Succulent blueberries and blackberries abound in August, and cherries and Concord grapes are also common. The brackish pond on West Head is one of only two Black-crowned Night Heron rookeries in the state.

There are future plans to redevelop Fort Andrews as an eco-retreat and family camp featuring yurts with electricity and water, allowing for more visitors to enjoy the history and natural beauty of Peddocks Island. Proposals to restore the chapel for wedding use and convert the cottages on Middle Head into an artist colony have also been discussed. What the future holds is unknown, but what is certain is that if the cottages disappear, the last connection to living history on the Boston Harbor Islands will be extinguished. Hopefully a solution can be found that will permit the roots of those who call Peddocks Island "home" to endure, while allowing new generations to create their own personal memories of this fascinating island.

ADDITIONAL INFORMATION

Private boaters should drop off guests and gear at the island dock and anchor offshore. A number of secure moorings are available through the Spectacle Island Marina. Call: 857-452-7221, or hail the Spectacle Island Marina on VHF 69. Reservations are advised.

To get to Peddocks from Long Wharf, take the free inter-island ferry from Georges Island. Consult crew onboard the mainland ferry. Ferry service also runs from Hingham Shipyard and Hull to Peddocks Island.

Bumpkin Island

Part of the charm and excitement of exploring the Boston Harbor Islands is that you never know what you will stumble upon. This is certainly the case with Bumpkin Island, where a grassy path through the woods leads to the remnants of an old stone farmhouse dating back to the early 1800s. Its round stones and arched doorways make it look as though it was plucked from the Irish countryside. The roof is gone, and its insides are overgrown with trees, but the outer shell has withstood the passing of about two hundred years, during which Bumpkin Island was transformed from farmland to home for a children's hospital to the site of a World War I naval training center.

Long before that, however, Native Americans traveled to Bumpkin Island during the summer months to dig for clams, hunt waterfowl, and gather fruits, nuts, and berries. Following the arrival of European settlers, the island was granted to Weymouth in 1636. At the time it was called Round Island. Like the rocks used to build the farmhouse, Bumpkin has an oval shape with a single sandbar snaking back toward Nantasket Peninsula.

In the mid-1600s, Samuel Ward obtained the island by royal grant. Upon his death, Ward bequeathed the island to Harvard College, thus providing the Boston Harbor Islands with a touch of the Ivy League. Ward gave the island to Harvard with the provision that it never be sold, although rental income could go to the college "for the easement of the charges of the diet of the students that are in the Commons." He also stipulated that the isle be known as Ward's Island. No such luck. Bumpkin stuck—maybe because it's just more fun to say than Ward's. (At times, the island has also been known as Bumkin, Bomkin, and Pumpkin.)

Throughout the next two centuries, Harvard leased Bumpkin Island for fifty dollars a year to tenant farmers. At the turn of the twentieth century, Albert Cameron Burrage—a wealthy lawyer, copper magnate, and civic leader—arranged to lease Bumpkin Island from Harvard for five hundred years.

Something of a renaissance man, Burrage remains an interesting figure in the city's history, and by the end of the nineteenth century he was highly regarded in Boston society. As a political and civic activist he served on the Boston Commerce Council and was the brains behind the Burrage Ordinance of 1892, which prohibited city employees from becoming involved in political action groups. Burrage was also appointed to the Boston Transit Commission, charged with the task of creating

The charming stone farmhouse on Bumpkin Island dates back to the early nineteenth century.

Boston's first subway system. A passion for horticulture (Burrage was renowned for the tropical orchids he cultivated) even led him to serve as president of the Massachusetts Horticultural Society for a period of time.

Burrage's tremendous success in business allowed him to live grandly, as shown by his chateau-style mansion at 314 Commonwealth Avenue. With its elaborate exterior stonework that includes dragons and gargoyles, the Burrage mansion remains an architectural highlight on any Back Bay tour today. Burrage's interest in Bumpkin, however, was solely in the name of philanthropy.

Bumpkin Island War Song

The November 3, 1918, edition of the Boston Sunday Advertiser included sheet music for new and popular songs to support the American cause in World War I. The featured song in the newspaper was "Bumkin Island" by the Boston Naval Reserves. Here are the lyrics that accompanied the music written by Mrs. G.L. Camden:

We sing of an isle that's a gem of the deep

Where sailors are made by the score

Where none but the hardiest sailor can keep a footing on its rock-bound shore

But we love it all the same and we love its dear old name

Though we work all the day rain or fair

So we'll learn to fight on the top of its height

Till we're called to the front over there

Bumkin Island! Bumkin Island!

The fairest spot in the sea

With the luster of the diamond

A spot where I love to be

Bumkin Island! Bumkin Island!

May your fame be spread a far

You're a jewel dropped from sky-land

For you'll help us win the war

We come from ev'ry walk and phase of life

All eager to respond to the call

With hardly any knowledge of military strife

And without much experience at all

But we're changing now from dubs to the men who'll down the subs

And we'll surely be a credit to your name

For we'll make the Hun take all hurdles on the run

And the Kaiser will be wiser at the game

Bumkin Island! Bumkin Island!

The fairest spot in the sea

With the luster of the diamond

A spot where I love to be

Bumkin Island! Bumkin Island!

May your fame be spread afar

You're a jewel dropped from sky-land

For you'll help us win the war

The Burrage Hospital, which opened in 1902, provided care and treatment for poor children with physical disabilities. Burrage had been awakened to the need for such a facility following a football injury that left his son confined to the house for weeks on end. While the hospital accepted children suffering from almost any non-contagious disease, particular attention was given to crippled and deformed children. According to *The Boston Daily Globe*, the island was an ideal place for the hospital because "its location is such that the cooling winds that always prevail here and the bright sunlight are depended upon to a great extent for cures."

The hospital dominated the crest of Bumpkin Island's drumlin, providing a commanding outlook from its perch seventy feet above the water. Charles Brigham, the architect who designed the old Museum of Fine Arts in Copley Square and Burrage's mansion, built the hospital with yellow brick, terra cotta, Indiana limestone trimmings, and a green slate roof. It was constructed in the shape of the letter H and equipped with wheelchair ramps to accommodate its patients. The children were able to enjoy the harbor views from a ten-foot-wide veranda running along its front.

The hospital could house as many as 150 children at a time. A daily steamer traveled between Boston and Bumpkin Island, and a doctor at the dock received patients and made arrangements for their stay. Parents were permitted to visit on Saturday, but only children could remain on the island.

Bumpkin Island was such an idyllic summer location that The Randidge Fund, another charitable endeavor in the early 1900s, sponsored daily island trips for poor children in Boston. Children spent the day on the island frolicking in the water, playing baseball, and enjoying picnics. In some years, the fund supported outings for as many as 15,000 children in a summer season.

As the United States prepared to enter World War I, Burrage closed the hospital and transferred his island lease to the federal government for the grand sum of one dollar a year. (To assist the war efforts, Burrage also lent the government his 260-foot steam yacht, the *Aztec*. Dismayed by the yacht's condition when it was returned to him after the war, Burrage filed a claim against the federal government and is said to have successfully recouped $300,000—of the $385,000 he'd requested —for repairs.)

The U.S. Navy took over Bumpkin Island as a naval training station, adding fifty-six temporary and wooden structures to the island by the end of 1917. The hospital building was transformed into naval headquarters and a sickbay. Toward the end of the war, German prisoners of war who had been held on Gallops Island (see page 62) were transferred to Bumpkin Island.

The naval station garrisoned upwards of 1,750 men at a time—a number on par with Fort Warren, Fort Andrews, and the other military instillations on the Boston Harbor Islands—and graduated nearly 15,000 seamen before the war was over. In

The Burrage mansion on Commonwealth Avenue, circa 1903. Courtesy the Library of Congress.

addition to their training, the enlisted men endeavored in other pursuits. In fact, music proved to be an important part of life for the reserves stationed on Bumpkin Island, with a twenty-three-piece band giving regular concerts on the veranda of the former hospital building. The sailors also played organized games of baseball and football. In 1917, a squad from Bumpkin Island squared off on the gridiron against Harvard University (the island's rightful owner) in Harvard Stadium. While the sailors lost 35-0, it's worth noting that Harvard was a pigskin power in the 1910s, eventually capturing four national championships during the decade.

When the war was over, almost all of the naval buildings were torn down or dismantled and rebuilt on shore. The cracked asphalt roads crossing the island are some of the few reminders of Bumpkin's days as a training station. On the north side of the island, near the shell of the old stone farmhouse, are the ruins of the station's mess hall. At its height, the mess fed all the Bumpkin Island troops in thirty minutes flat.

The dock at Bumpkin Island contains an outdoor exhibit area. The stone building to the right served as a pump house for the naval training station.

Chunks of concrete have crumbled to the ground, poison ivy and other plants climb the remaining walls, the terrazzo floor is no more, and the roof is missing—but close your eyes and you can hear the music, the clinking silverware, and the lively mealtime chatter masking the certain dread trainees must have felt about their pending trips to the front.

The Navy left Bumpkin Island after the war and Burrage's hospital reopened only for a brief time in the summer of 1940, when it treated children with polio. In 1946, the hospital was destroyed by a spectacular blaze, visible for more than ten miles around. Today, the hospital site looks as if a river of red and yellow bricks swept in to flood an open pit. Within this sea of bricks only small sections of the hospital's edifice remain intact. The spruce trees, which once guided patients and visitors to the hospital's grand entrance, now serve to conceal what remains of the structure. (Watch out for poison ivy if you decide to explore the ruins.)

Like many of the harbor islands, centuries of agricultural use left Bumpkin Island bleak and treeless. (In fact, Frederick Law Olmsted had proposed a reforestation plan for the Boston Harbor Islands, including Bumpkin, in the 1890s. See page 197.) Today, the scene is much different. Invasive species and trees planted around the hospital grounds have filled in the landscape, and Bumpkin Island, like Grape, is brimming with blackberries, bayberries, dewberries, raspberries, and elderberries. Summer sees pink and white sea roses and yellow wildflowers, set against staghorn sumac, gray birch, and quaking aspen. Pear and apple trees can also be found along the island's paths.

Bumpkin Island has long been a popular place for picnickers, and the picnic area, situated in a wide expanse on the island's southwest corner, provides a picturesque view of Hingham Bay and Slate and Grape Islands. Campgrounds are available off the long straight path that bisects the island.

It is on the north side of Bumpkin Island that you will be treated to its most spectacular vista. There, the Boston skyline is perfectly framed by the Middle and East Head of Peddocks Island. Rising from the tombolo connecting those heads, the soaring edifices that form the backbone of the city reach for the sky. It's a great place to enjoy the restorative summer breezes that attracted Burrage and so many others through the years to Bumpkin Island.

ADDITIONAL INFORMATION

 Ranger-led edible berry walks. An annual art encampment features performance art and mixed-media installations by local artists inspired by the harbor islands.

Reservations are required to camp on Bumpkin Island and can be made online at www.ReserveAmerica.com or call toll-free 877-422-6762. Your camping reservation is not site specific. At check-in an island ranger will assign you a campsite. The camping season runs from late June to early September.

For boaters arriving by private craft, docks are for drop-off only.

 To get to Bumpkin from Long Wharf, take the free inter-island ferry from Georges Island. Consult crew onboard mainland ferry. Ferry service also runs from Hingham Shipyard and Hull to Bumpkin Island.

Grape Island

A few steps from the dock on Grape Island, a set of inviting Adirondack chairs beckon from under the shady canopy of a soaring evergreen. It is a fitting welcome to this picturesque, secluded island. Unlike many of the Boston Harbor Islands, the fifty acres that make up Grape Island have been spared the scars left by the large-scale construction of forts, hospitals, and social institutions. It is this nearly pristine environment that makes Grape Island the finest camping island in the harbor and an unparalleled draw for nature lovers. Grape Island is *the* place to get away from it all, reconnect with the great outdoors, and feel as if you are in the woods of northern New England, rather than eight miles from downtown Boston.

With a name like Grape Island, you might expect to see a landscape teeming with tangled vines. While the island is said to have received its name from the wild grapes that once attracted European settlers, there are none on the island today. (Though, a grape arbor near the dock is a nod to the island's name, not to mention the perfect place to wait for the ferry on a hot day.) What you will find, however, is an island filled with a wide variety of interesting flora and fauna that you could spend hours exploring.

Native Americans were drawn to Grape Island for thousands of years. In the 1800s, tomahawks were commonly discovered on the island, and in the 1970s archaeologists unearthed a midden—a large waste deposit of shells and refuse left behind by indigenous peoples. Lack of development on Grape Island over the years means there is the potential for other archaeological finds in the future.

After the Europeans arrived, the island was primarily used for farming and grazing, with the last permanent residents of Grape Island leaving in the 1940s. A foundation of a nineteenth-century farmhouse near the dock is one of the few remaining signs of the island's agricultural past. The farmhouse also served as the island caretaker's cottage during the first half of the twentieth century, when the island was owned by the Bradley Fertilizer Company, which had a large operation across the channel on Weymouth Neck. The fertilizer company used the island to graze horses and harvest hay for the Bradley family polo grounds in Hingham. Those polo grounds eventually became the Hingham Shipyard, which contributed over 227 ships, largely Destroyer Escorts, to the war efforts during World War II. The rich history of the Hingham Shipyard remains a significant source of pride for South Shore residents today.

It was the agricultural use of Grape Island that triggered the island's most notable historic event—a colorful armed skirmish during the Revolutionary War. While every school-age child is familiar with the battles at Lexington and Concord that launched the American fight for independence, very few realize that the next armed confrontation between the British and Boston colonists wasn't at Bunker Hill. It was at Grape Island.

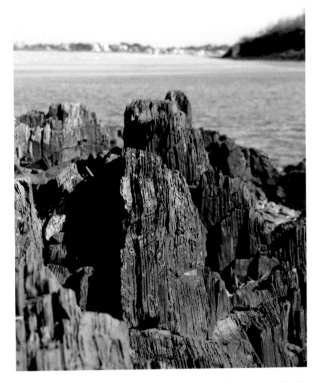

Following the devastating battles at Lexington and Concord, the beleaguered British troops and their sympathizers found themselves under siege and holed up on the peninsula of Boston in desperate need of supplies. With land routes cut off, the British set their sights on the farms of the Boston Harbor Islands, which remained readily available to them as their naval supremacy remained intact.

Some of the slate bedrock that underlies Boston Harbor is visible on Grape Island.

It was on the morning of May 21, 1775—a little more than a month after the battles at Lexington and Concord and a little less than a month before the battle at Bunker Hill—that the Grape Island Alarm began. That morning, a small British force set out in four boats for the island with the hopes of seizing cattle, vegetables, and hay for horses and livestock. At the time, Grape Island was owned by Elisha Leavitt, a Loyalist living in Hingham. Old Elisha offered up his farm's provisions to the British army, thereby becoming, in the eyes of his patriot neighbors, a turncoat for the redcoats.

British boats sailing toward the south shore of Boston Harbor were a troubling sight to the colonists, and wild rumors quickly spread that as many as three hundred redcoats were launching an attack on Hingham, Weymouth, or another neighboring town. General alarms began to sound. Bells pealed and guns fired to rouse the militia. When the patriots finally arrived at Weymouth Neck, they discovered the British weren't attempting a land invasion as feared, but loading their boats with hay from Leavitt's farm across the channel.

The good news for the revolutionaries was that the British force was much smaller than originally reported. The bad news was that the militia had arrived at low tide and was therefore forced to wait until the flats were covered by the flood tide in order to launch their boats. The colonists anxiously watched for hours as the British made the long trip from barn to boat and back again, carting Leavitt's hay as they went. To make matters more vexing, the distance across the water was too great for the militia's small arms to be of any use. They fired in vain anyway, with the British vessels returning fire as their troops worked. Finally the tide was high enough for the colonists to attack—but no sooner had the Americans launched their boats, than the British returned to their ships and set sail for Boston with the few tons of hay they had successfully removed. The colonists, exchanging fire with the retreating redcoats, landed on Grape Island and proceeded to burn Leavitt's barn to the ground, along with its remaining seventy to eighty tons of hay. Leavitt's cattle were spared but relocated to the mainland.

An angry mob of patriots set out for Leavitt's house in Hingham to exact retribution, but catching wind of their coming, Elisha was ready. Not with a rifle, it is said, but with cheese and crackers, cake, and a barrel of rum. The refreshments did the trick and calmed the patriots. After all, who wouldn't trade a little hay for some spirits and light fare?

The bucolic atmosphere on Grape Island today provides no hint to the confused events that took place on that day more than two hundred years ago. After the last resident left and the agricultural use of the island ceased, Grape Island developed into a woody, shrubby landscape. Grassy paths loop around the circumference and down the middle of the island. At certain spots, the trails are walled in by bushes measuring more than five feet high. Numerous benches provide wonderful harbor views, although some vistas are becoming obscured by growing foliage.

Unless you're a budding arborist, be sure to grab a copy of the park brochure, which provides a self-guided tour with commentary on the island's diverse flora. Like many of the Boston Harbor Islands, Grape Island is filled with staghorn sumac, so named because their hairy upper stems and flower stalks resemble a deer's velvety antlers. Staghorn sumac, whose fuzzy red berries can be harvested to brew a cold

Letter from Abigail Adams; Braintree, Massachusetts
May 24, 1775

"I suppose you have had a formidable account of the alarm we had last Sunday morning. When I rose, about six o'clock, I was told that the drums had been some time beating, and that three alarm guns were fired, that Weymouth bell had been ringing, and Mr. Weld's was then ringing.

"I immediately sent off an express to know the occasion, and found the whole town in confusion. Three sloops and one cutter had come out and dropped anchor just below Great Hill. It was difficult to tell their designs; some supposed they were coming to Germantown [in Braintree], others to Weymouth; people, women, children from the iron works came flocking down this way—every woman and child above or from below my father's. My father's family flying, the Drs. [Dr. Cotton Tufts's] in great distress, as you may well imagine for my aunt had her bed thrown into a cart, into which she got herself, and ordered the boy to drive her off to Bridgewater, which he did.

"The report was to them that three hundred had landed, and were upon their march into town. The alarm flew like lightning, and men from all parts came flocking down, until two thousand were collected. But it seems their expedition was to Grape Island for Leavitt's hay. There it was impossible to reach them, for want of boats; but the sight of so many persons, and the firing at them, prevented their getting more than three tons of hay, though they had carted much more down to the water.

Abigail Adams was one of the colonists roused by the Grape Island Alarm. John Adams, who would become the country's second president, was away from the couple's saltbox house in present-day Quincy to attend the Second Continental Congress in Philadelphia. Their letters to each other provide a window into some of the early confusion and fear about the intent of the British forces.

"At last they mustered a lighter, and a sloop from Hingham, which had six port-holes. Our men eagerly jumped on board, and put off for the island. As soon as they perceived it, they decamped. Our people landed upon the island, and in an instant set fire to the hay, which, with the barn, was soon consumed, about eighty tons, it is said. We expect soon to be in continual alarms, until something decisive takes place."

Letter from John Adams; Philadelphia, Pennsylvania
June 10, 1775

"I long to know, how you fare, and whether you are often discomposed with alarms. Guard yourself against them, my dear. I think you are in no danger—don't let the groundless fears, and fruitful imaginations of others affect you. Let me know what guards are kept—and

who were principally concerned in the battle at Grape Island, as well as that at Chelsea. The reputation of our countrymen for valor is very high. I hope they will maintain it, as well as that for prudence, caution, and conduct."

Letter from Abigail Adams; Braintree, Massachusetts
June 22, 1775

"You inquire of me who were at the engagement at Grape Island. I may say with truth, all Weymouth, Braintree, Hingham, who were able to bear arms, and hundreds from other towns within twenty, thirty, and forty miles of Weymouth... Both your brothers were there; your younger brother [Elihu], with his company, who gained honor by their good order that day. He was one of the first to venture aboard a schooner to land upon the island."

drink called sumac-ade, is considered a pioneer species on the harbor islands as it is among the first plants to return to an area that was disturbed by activities such as fire, agriculture, and deforestation. Groves of other early successional species such as gray birch and quaking aspen also cover the island.

Although a visit to Grape Island would be delightful any time of year, the island explodes with color from its profusion of wild berries during the summer—including six edible varieties. Thanks to these berry bushes, Grape Island is a haven for wildlife. The berries attract a wide variety of birds, such as songbirds, quail, and pheasant. Visitors to the island may also encounter deer, rabbits, and—hold your nose—skunks.

Grape Island lies just five hundred yards offshore from Weymouth Neck and is composed of two drumlins connected by a marshy lowland. The island's west drumlin is the larger of the two, rising seventy feet above sea level. Three shaded benches on this side of the island provide an expansive view of the harbor and the city from the John F. Kennedy Library in Dorchester all the way to the Bunker Hill Monument in Charlestown.

A boat ashore Grape Island, with Slate Island in the distance.

On the north side of Grape Island paths lead to a stony beach that has the look and feel of a secluded cove; the long, curved shoreline will have you wondering why you didn't bring your beach chair and umbrella. The rocky beach on the east side of the island is filled with the colorful shells of blue mussels, white soft-shell clams, and periwinkles.

The south side of the island is home to a marshy lowland that contains plants such as salt-spray roses, salt-water cordgrass, and seaside goldenrod. Some of the slate bedrock that underlies Boston Harbor is visible as an outcrop on this side of the island. Marsh wildflowers, such as seaside goldenrod, jimson weed, beach pea, and scarlet pimpernel, can be found near the beach.

Grape Island's natural surroundings make it the best camping experience on the Boston Harbor Islands. Its wooded campsites are away from the visitor paths, providing some privacy. While other islands such as Bumpkin and Lovells have noteworthy remnants of human development, camping on Grape Island will really make you feel like you're roughing it. And there's one added benefit of camping on Grape Island. Those Adirondack chairs are even more inviting come sunset.

ADDITIONAL INFORMATION

 Reservations are required to camp on Grape Island and can be made online at www.ReserveAmerica.com or call toll-free 877-422-6762. Your camping reservation is not site specific. At check-in, an island ranger will assign you a campsite. The camping season runs from late June to early September.

For boaters arriving by private craft, docks are for drop-off only.

 Ranger-led bird walks and kayak expeditions held in summer months.

 To get to Grape from Long Wharf, take the free inter-island ferry from Georges Island. Ferry service also runs from Hingham Shipyard and Hull to Grape Island.

Hangman Island

The haunting name of desolate Hangman Island is apropos. Hangman Island is composed of rugged granite and slate rocks, which Bostonians quarried in colonial times. Coupled with the eroding power of the sea, the removal of the island's stone reduced Hangman Island to less than an acre in size at high tide. Only three feet above sea level, its low elevation can make the island difficult to spot when the tide is high.

Located in Quincy Bay due west of Peddocks, the exact origin of Hangman Island's appellation is unknown. According to one legend, pirates were executed and hung up in gibbets on the island, though there is no historical records to prove it. Another story has it that a hermit living on the island also served as the county hangman.

What is known is that Hangman Island was a seasonal home in the late 1800s and early 1900s to a handful of fishermen and lobstermen, who lived in modest, wooden shacks; and they were known to courageously answer the distress calls of mariners in the harbor surrounding the island.

The only residents on Hangman Island these days are gulls, ducks, and other seabirds. A small, pebbly beach on the southern side offers a landing spot, but Hangman Island is difficult to approach because of the many rocks and hidden shoals in the immediate area.

Sheep Island

While out photographing the islands, Sherman "Pat" Morss, Jr., (see page 156) discovered these chickens — a curious throwback to the island's colonial days as a pasture for grazing sheep.

It's hard to imagine looking at it today, but in colonial times, Sheep Island was a sizable plot of land. The island was once twenty-five acres in size and large enough to be used for grazing sheep, hence its name. But centuries of pounding wind and water have reduced Sheep Island to a sliver of land between Grape and Peddocks Islands, measuring just a few acres.

During the late 1800s and early 1900s, the island was used for recreational outings, including an annual trip by members of the Sheep Island Club, which included prominent Boston politicians and businessmen. Each year, the club sailed to Sheep Island, set up a tent, and enjoyed an afternoon feast of chowder. Apparently, this was quite an affair. It took about five hours to cook the chowder, eat the chowder, "talk the chowder over," and go home. Decades later, Sheep Island was a less hospitable place for pleasure seekers. A hermit reportedly lived on the island and it was said he'd shoot anyone daring to land on its shores.

Covered by scrubby vegetation, sumacs, and marsh grass, the island is accessed by beach landing, but there is little to see. It is a nesting site for birds, and visitation is discouraged during nesting season because birds can be aggressive—although perhaps not as combative as a gun-toting hermit.

Slate Island

Slate Island, from Grape Island.

Even though it lies just 250 yards east of Grape Island, Slate Island is geologically different than its neighbor. Grape Island is composed of two glacial drumlins, while Slate Island consists of slate outcrops.

As early as the 1600s, the island's slate was used in the construction of houses in and around Puritan Boston. Nathaniel Bradstreet Shurtleff, an author and mayor of Boston between 1868 and 1870, wrote in *A Topographical and Historical Description of Boston* that "although the material has not been of a remarkable quality for the protection of roofs, it has done good service for underpinning and for cellar walls." The blue-colored slate was also used to make some of the gravestones that can be seen in Hingham Cemetery today, and remnants of the quarrying activity can still be found on the island. In the 1930s, the Davis Bates Clapp Memorial Association, a charitable nonprofit organization, ran a short-lived summer camp for boys on Slate Island.

A rocky beach on the island's southwestern shore is a good landing spot for kayaks and flat-bottomed boats, but the lack of trails, dense underbrush, and poison ivy make it difficult to explore the island's twelve-acre interior.

Raccoon Island

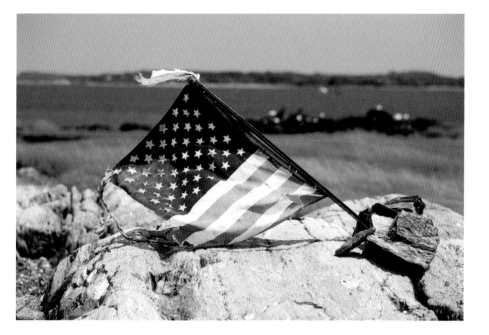

Tiny Raccoon Island, little more than three acres in size, lies just two hundred yards off the shore of Quincy's Houghs Neck peninsula. This bedrock outcropping in Hingham Bay is so close to shore that it is accessible across the mudflats at low tide.

Many colorful characters have lived on the Boston Harbor Islands over the years, but Clifford H. Jenks, who bought Raccoon Island in 1923, was undoubtedly one of the more eccentric. According to *The Boston Globe*, Jenks was known as "the Human Fly," an appellation he earned by scaling the sides of buildings.

Shortly after buying Raccoon Island, Jenks tried to perform another daring feat—he wanted to bring his car to the island from the mainland. Unfortunately, the car got stuck in the mudflats. Ever resourceful, Jenks tied empty barrels to the car and managed to float it the rest of the way at high tide. Of course, the more interesting story might be *why* Jenks needed a car on the tiny island in the first place.

Hingham Harbor Islands

On summer weekends, Hingham Harbor is awash with sea-going vessels of all shapes and sizes. Kayakers paddle across the blue sheet of water, sailors hoist billowing sails, and yacht owners carry on the town's proud nautical tradition while listening to the Red Sox game on the radio.

Hingham has always been a seafaring town, built on the backs of the fishing and shipbuilding industries. During Hingham's maritime heyday in the nineteenth century, it was common to gaze upon wooden mackerel fishing fleets heading out to sea or yachts racing in fevered competition. Magnificent steamers, some of them capable of carrying as many as 1,500 people, plied the harbor on their routes between Hingham, Boston, and Nantasket.

While the types of sea craft have changed over the centuries, one constant in Hingham Harbor has been its four picturesque islands—Button, Langlee, Sarah, and Ragged. And these small, rocky islands, owned by the town of Hingham, are pleasant spots to explore. All four islands are in close proximity and can easily be visited in a morning or afternoon, and they are particularly popular with kayakers, who can launch from the town beach on Hingham Harbor.

RAGGED ISLAND	SARAH ISLAND
Latitude: 42° 15' 26.0" North	Latitude: 42° 15' 27.8" North
Longitude: 70° 53' 26.0" West	Longitude: 70° 53' 08.21" West

LANGLEE ISLAND	BUTTON ISLAND
Latitude: 42° 15' 39.0" North	Latitude: 42° 15' 3.4" North
Longitude: 70° 53' 15.4" West	Longitude: 70° 53' 4.4" West

According to local folklore, Hingham resident John Langley named the three northernmost islands in the harbor (Sarah, Ragged, and Langlee) after his beautiful, but raggedly dressed daughter Sarah. While Langley did own these islands in the late 1600s, the legend that he lived on the islands as a poor fisherman is apparently untrue. In reality, Langley was an innkeeper and a boatyard owner, although Sarah and her friends probably spent summer days playing on the islands. John Langley's daughter grew up to be Sarah Langley Derby, who in 1784 endowed one of the oldest coeducational private schools in the United States-—Hingham's venerable Derby Academy.

Although you would never know it today, another Hingham institution once occupied the harbor's western shore. For a quarter of a century, Hingham's Crow Point neighborhood was home to Melville Garden, one of New England's finest resorts in the late nineteenth century. Wealthy Boston industrialist Samuel Downer, who built his fortune in the kerosene business, spent a quarter of a million dollars to turn his private estate, located along present-day Downer Avenue, into an enchanting pleasure ground. Although a teetotaler himself, Downer modeled his amusement park after the German beer gardens that so captivated him on his European travels.

As many as seventy thousand people visited Melville Garden each summer between 1871 and 1896. Eleven times a day, steamboats would depart from Boston's Rowes Wharf with visitors eager to leave the hot, crowded city to enjoy the refreshing sea breezes and amusements at Melville Garden. Park patrons could take a leisurely stroll around the beautiful grounds and its fine Victorian buildings. If they wanted a little more activity, they could take a swim, fish, shoot billiards, row around the harbor, play croquet, and listen to bands play in the music hall. For fifty cents, visitors could stuff themselves at the Rhode Island clam bake pavilion, which could seat more than a thousand diners at a time. Children were thrilled by the garden's "flying horses," Punch-and-Judy shows, and monkey cages. There was even a bear den.

After sunset, park patrons were amazed by the wonder of Melville Garden's twenty electric lights, the first in Hingham. And fireworks lit up the night sky every Tuesday and Thursday. At the end of the night, visitors could either take a steamer back to Boston or spend the night at the ornate eighty-room Rose Standish House.

Another popular attraction for visitors to Melville Garden was the ferry boat to nearby Ragged Island, the westernmost isle in Hingham Harbor. The views from the island's gazebos, pavilions, and lookouts made it a popular picnicking spot for parasol-toting women and men nattily attired in their suits and bowler hats.

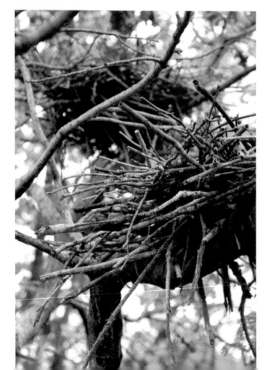

Today, Ragged Island is no longer a place to visit dressed in your Sunday best. Much of Ragged Island's interior is impenetrable due to overgrown brambles, and steep rock ledges surrounding the island make it difficult to circumnavigate. There is a small rocky cove on the island's northeast side on which to come ashore. Watch out for poison ivy and the thickets that will have you thinking "jagged" would have been a more appropriate name for the island.

East of Ragged Island, Sarah Island offers a better opportunity for exploration.

Sarah Island is a popular nesting spot for gulls, egrets, cormorants, and herons.

A gravelly beach on the north side of the island offers the best location to come ashore, as thirty-foot-high ledges flank the island's southern shore. Adjacent to the beach are mudflats filled with salt grass and large tidal pools that resemble water-filled craters. While there are no trails, Sarah Island is more passable than Ragged, though there is considerable undergrowth on the western side of the island.

Sarah Island, once known as Sailor's Island before its purchase by John Langley, is a popular nesting spot for gulls, egrets, cormorants, and herons. In the springtime, the birds' chorus rises from the rookeries and fills the air around the island. Keep in mind that visitation to Sarah Island is greatly discouraged during nesting season, as birds tend to be very territorial.

John R. Brewer, the owner of World's End, purchased Sarah and Langlee Islands in 1860 for the sum of $250. At that time, the islands, like World's End, were barren landmasses. In the early 1890s, Brewer planted trees at World's End according to plans drawn up by Frederick Law Olmsted (see page 193); he extended the reforestation to his two islands. Numerous maples, oaks, elms, and cedars that were planted by Brewer's employees remain on Sarah Island today.

On Langlee Island, the leafy canopy of these now-mature oaks, maples, and cedars offer welcome shade. A picnic table below a grand old oak tree in the middle of the island is particularly inviting. There are no paths on Langlee Island, but thanks to its mature woodlands, it is the easiest of the Hingham Harbor islands to explore.

A small beach on the northwest side of Langlee Island offers a place to come ashore. Above the beach is a forty-foot-high cliff of Roxbury puddingstone that provides the best vantage point in Hingham Harbor. This outlook offers views of the harbor from nearby Crow Point to downtown Boston in the distance. Make sure to check out the view beneath your feet, too. Roxbury pud-

The Hingham Yacht Club.

dingstone is a conglomerate composed of rocks of all different shapes, sizes, and colors cemented together by geological forces. The end result is something that looks a little like Christmas pudding. Unless you're a geologist, you probably didn't know that Roxbury puddingstone is the state rock of Massachusetts. (But be honest—did you even know there *is* a state rock?)

Low tide is an interesting time to explore Langlee Island's tidal mudflats, filled with hermit crabs, barnacles, and eelgrass, on its western side. The southeast shore of Langlee Island includes a sweeping sandbar and sandy beach, which offers another spot to come ashore.

Button Island, the southernmost island in Hingham Harbor, received its name because of its diminutive size of less than an acre. There are no trails on Button Island and not much to see besides a handful of trees and dense undergrowth of brambles. Getting ashore can be a challenge since the island is bounded by small rock outcrops, boulders, sand, and mudflats.

Thousands of revelers are drawn to the shores of Hingham Harbor around the Fourth of July to watch the fireworks launched from Button Island. The patriotic pyrotechnics hark back to the shows that lit up the night sky above the harbor and Melville Garden more than a century ago. The flying horses, wondrous Victorian buildings, and bear den may be long gone, but the Hingham Harbor islands are still there for our recreation and entertainment.

Natural Wonders

Roxbury puddingstone — the state rock of Massachusetts.

With the loss of biodiversity on the planet at an all-time high, we can turn to the Boston Harbor Islands as a treasure trove of information about how nature maintains an abundance and diversity of plant and animal life in miniature "worlds." We can also study the different stages of natural succession—where one wild community transforms over years and decades into another—and how human activities can disturb or restore these communities.

Currently, much of the harbor islands' flora and fauna has been documented. Dozens of habitats—from forests to woodlands to rocky shores and a variety of marine communities—have been studied in great depth. Enormous surveys have recorded over five hundred species of plants, over one hundred species of birds, and nearly four hundred species of invertebrates. Small mammals and snakes have been recorded, as have our creepy crawly friends—the insects, spiders, millipedes, and centipedes.

Much of the diversity found on the islands, however, is due to changes in habitat caused by deforestation or the introduction of invasive species. Native Americans likely used the islands as a base for harvesting coastal resources, such as fish and shellfish, but may have planted crops and introduced new species to the islands. European settlers deforested much of the remaining native forests, introduced agricultural crops, grazing animals, and even weeds, dramatically transforming the landscape as early as the late seventeenth century.

Invasive species pose a great threat to natural communities and are one of the major priorities of conservation and restoration activity of park managers. Invasive plants replace the native tree species, resulting in a different three-dimensional structure and light environment for the forest or woodlands. This can have consequences for the native animals that rely on the forest for food or breeding. Likewise, exotic animals pose threats to native plants and animals. Exotic species have not co-evolved with the communities in which they live and therefore are often not subjected to predation or the natural diseases that limit the growth of native populations. Once established, invasive species can fundamentally alter the local ecosystem. As park managers eradicate these exotics, native vegetation can reclaim its territory, much as it reclaims the ruins of bygone structures dotting the islands.

A collaboration between the Museum of Comparative Zoology at Harvard and the Boston Harbor Islands Partnership has spawned yet another great effort to explore the natural history of the islands: The All Taxa Biodiveristy Inventory (ATBI). Their mission is to record the "microwilderness" of the islands—those creeping, crawling, multi-legged critters mentioned previously. While many of the larger mammals, birds, and plants of pre-European contact are now gone, these smaller creatures remain largely unaffected after thousands of years. This project offers great insight into island biogeography as well as an educational opportunity for the public, as enthusiasts are encouraged to participate in the data collection and analysis.

In fact, citizen science and other stewardship-driven activities are an important component within the management structure of the park. Nature groups and individuals can participate in many activities, from restoration of native habitats to the "bio blitzes" associated with the ATBI. Nature may have formed the islands, but it is up to citizens to protect, restore, and reclaim the benefits that come from a healthy environment. With public support, park management can continue to provide a vibrant, biologically rich resource from drumlin top to shaley shore, for the benefit of those who value scientific discovery, hands-on education, and the chance to get a little lost in the wilderness.

—*Marah Hardt, Ph.D.*

For more information visit:
www.nps.gov/boha

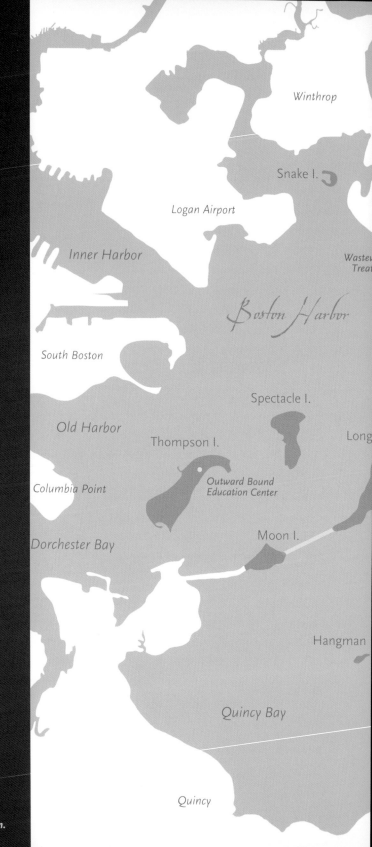

Winthrop

Snake I.

Logan Airport

Inner Harbor

Wastev
Trea

Boston Harbor

South Boston

Spectacle I.

Old Harbor

Long

Thompson I.

Columbia Point

Outward Bound
Education Center

Dorchester Bay

Moon I.

Hangman

Quincy Bay

Quincy

Map not intended for navigation.

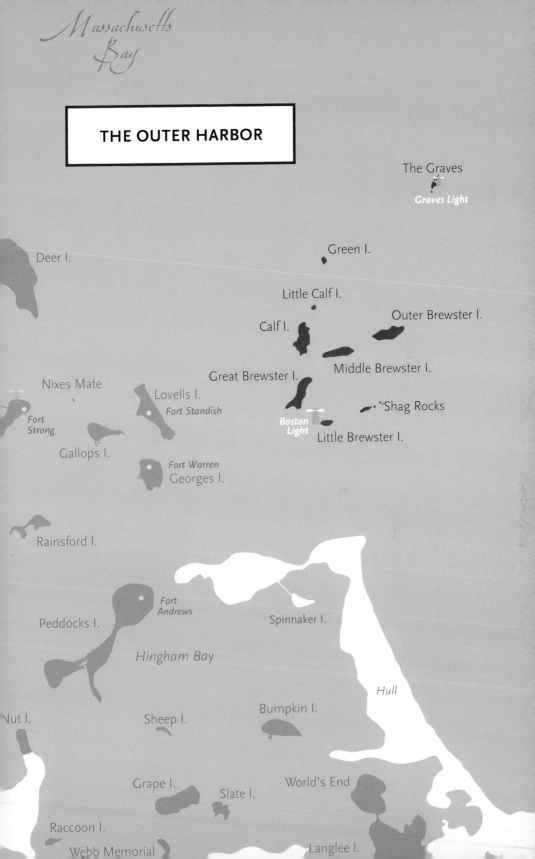

Massachusetts Bay

THE OUTER HARBOR

The Graves

Graves Light

Deer I.

Green I.

Little Calf I.

Outer Brewster I.

Calf I.

Nixes Mate

Lovells I.

Fort Standish

Great Brewster I.

Middle Brewster I.

Fort Strong

Boston Light

Shag Rocks

Gallops I.

Little Brewster I.

Fort Warren

Georges I.

Rainsford I.

Fort Andrews

Peddocks I.

Spinnaker I.

Hingham Bay

Hull

Nut I.

Sheep I.

Bumpkin I.

Grape I.

Slate I.

World's End

Raccoon I.

Webb Memorial

Langlee I.

Little Brewster Island

As the ferry docks at Little Brewster Island, it is met by Sally Snowman, keeper of Boston Light, clad in an eighteenth-century costume. Her hand-sewn colonial dress and white bonnet recalls the romantic days of lighthouses. Snowman's warm reception is appropriate for an island and lighthouse that has welcomed storm-tossed mariners from distant shores for nearly three hundred years.

Little Brewster Island, the smallest of the Brewsters, is a rocky island barely more than an acre in size. What it lacks in size, however, it makes up for in stature. This humble island is dominated by the distinguished, bold pillar of Boston Light, a postcard-perfect New England lighthouse. As the first light station built in the U.S., Boston Light is not only the most historic structure on the Boston Harbor Islands, but also a revered National Historic Landmark.

In colonial days, the primary entrance to the harbor was between Little Brewster Island and Point Allerton on the northern reach of Hull. Navigating the entrance could be tricky, particularly for captains unfamiliar with the harbor's layout. Before Boston Light, crude navigation beacons—some mere lanterns or lit bales of pitch hung from tall poles—were erected on Hull and the harbor islands as early as the 1670s. Inevitably, the lack of a reliable navigation aid threatened the safety of the crews and cargos of trade ships, along with the city's maritime supremacy.

In 1713, John George, Jr., a prominent Boston merchant, petitioned the Massachusetts legislature to build a permanent lighthouse at the entrance of the harbor to prevent the loss of lives and goods, ensure the seaport's continued growth, and provide Boston with a competitive advantage against commercial rivals such as New York City. After surveying potential sights, it was determined that Little Brewster Island, known at the time as Beacon Island—presumably because of those makeshift nautical beacons—would be the best site for the lighthouse.

With construction delayed by disagreements over how it would be financed, Boston Light wasn't kindled until September 14, 1716. But what a triumph it was for Boston when those first beams bounced across the waves of Massachusetts Bay! Not only was Boston Light the first lighthouse in North America, it was one of only a few lighthouses to be found anywhere in the world at that time.

A tax of a penny a ton on all vessels entering and leaving the harbor was levied to pay for Boston Light. The lighthouse tower was approximately sixty feet high and made of stone, although there was considerable woodwork around the structure and lantern frame. This woodwork made it susceptible to fire, as was the case in 1720 and 1751 when fires badly damaged the light.

In addition to aiding mariners, Boston Light protected Boston from attack. If the keeper sighted enemy ships approaching, he would signal the fort at Castle Island by hoisting and lowering the Union Jack as many times as there were ships approaching. The Castle would then provide a similar signal to the town. If more than four or five ships were approaching, however, the Castle fired three warning shots so that the governor could alert surrounding towns of possible attack by lighting the signal atop Beacon Hill.

If you let your imagination roam free for a moment, you can easily picture how arduous life was for the early keepers of Boston Light, many of whom had homes and farms on the harbor islands. Light keepers needed to do much more than just ensure

As a little girl growing up in Weymouth, Sally Snowman fell in love with Boston Light. As an adult, she became an auxiliary member of the Coast Guard, developing interpretive programs and writing a book on the lighthouse along with her husband. When the time came to select the seventieth keeper of Boston Light in 2003, Sally was a natural choice.

"Boston Harbor and the islands were my playground when I was growing up. We had sailboats, a powerboat, and a rowboat. I have seawater in my veins, so if I'm away from the water too long, I get very crabby. My dad brought me out to Boston Light when I was ten years old, and I instantaneously connected with it. I just knew that I'd like to get married out here one day, and in 1994 I did! The thought of being a keeper was a fantasy, and to think that my fantasy came true is phenomenal.

"Every day I just feel so fortunate that I'm here. I am so honored and humbled by the trust put in me to manage the oldest Coast Guard light station in the country.

"The energy of this island talks to me. It did when I was ten years old, and it still talks to me now. When you open the windows of the house, you hear the cawing of the seagulls, the bell buoys out in the harbor, and the squeal of the hydraulics from the lobstermen bringing up their traps. I keep coming out and taking pictures of the goldenrod, the monarch butterflies, and the chicory. It's just beautiful.

"Visitors come and experience the island on whatever level they want. They can look at it as a lighthouse, metaphorically the beacon of light and the salvation of the shipwrecked. Or it could just be the architecture. Others just love the concept of lighthouses and islands. So everyone is drawn to come and visit this place for various reasons. We all connect with this island."

The grave of George Worthylake, who is buried with his wife and daughter in Copp's Hill.

that the flames were lit through all kinds of weather. They also had to keep the lamp lenses and lantern glass clean, respond to fog signals from vessels, act as health officers in case of sickness onboard incoming vessels, and occasionally entertain unexpected guests. The first guardians of the light supplemented their incomes by renting themselves out as harbor pilots, and many brave keepers risked their own lives to rescue shipwreck survivors.

The fate of the first two keepers of Boston Light underscores the hazards of working in the outer harbor. On November 3, 1718, George Worthylake, the first keeper of Boston Light, was returning from Boston in a sloop with his family, their servant, and a friend. Near the island, Worthylake dropped anchor and the party was met by Worthylake's slave, Shadwell, who had rowed out in a canoe. On their approach to the island, the canoe capsized, and everyone aboard drowned. Worthylake, his wife, and daughter are buried underneath a triple headstone in the Copp's Hill Burying Ground in the North End. Incredibly, Worthylake's temporary replacement, Robert Saunders, drowned in stormy weather just a few days later, before his appointment was even confirmed. The terrible incident was big news in Boston, and it inspired a twelve-year-old Benjamin Franklin to write a poetic account, entitled *The Lighthouse Tragedy*, which he hawked around the docks and streets of Boston.

In the battle for American independence, Boston Light was a strategic target for both the colonists and the British. During the siege of Boston in 1775, the British still controlled the harbor and its lighthouse. On the morning of July 20, 1775, Major Joseph Vose and a detachment of colonial soldiers launched a raid on Little Brewster Island. The patriots burned the wooden parts of the lighthouse and removed three casks of oil, gunpowder, and furniture.

Protected by a guard of marines, the British quickly deployed Loyalist workers to repair Boston Light. But just eleven days after the first attack, the patriots struck again. This time, a detachment of three hundred men led by Major Benjamin Tupper landed on the island in the early morning hours. They overcame the guard and destroyed the structures being erected. Tupper's men killed between ten and twelve British troops and made prisoners of the rest, suffering only one fatality of their own. In his General

Orders of August 1, 1775, General George Washington thanked Major Tupper and his men "for their gallant and soldier-like behavior in possessing themselves of the enemy's post at the light-house and for the number of prisoners they took there."

Fast forward to June 1776. Though the British had evacuated Boston, their ships still lurked in the harbor, where, as the October 1895 edition of the *New England Magazine* colorfully put it, they "contented themselves for a time in doing all the mischief they could upon the several islands within it." When they were finally driven from the city's waters for good on June 13, the British returned the favor. The redcoats used a timed charge to blow up the tower of Boston Light. Because of this ignominious "parting gift," the beacon at Sandy Hook, New Jersey, dating to 1764, has the distinction of being the "oldest" lighthouse structure in America. However, Bostonians can still take comfort in the fact that Boston Light remains the oldest "light station" in the United States.

Boston Light was dark for seven years before it was rebuilt under orders from John Hancock in 1783. The new conical tower of brick and granite was seventy-five feet topped by an octagonal lantern fifteen feet high. In 1859, the tower was raised fourteen feet to accommodate a new Fresnel lens imported from France, allowing its white light to shine twenty-seven miles out to sea.

Since its earliest days, Boston Light has been a guide for thousands of sea vessels, but in September 1910, during the Harvard-Boston Aero Meet, the lighthouse served as a landmark for another mode of transportation. Today, planes traveling to and from Logan Airport are familiar sights in the skies above the islands, but in 1910 few Bostonians had ever seen an airplane in

Start of the race to Boston Light, during the Harvard-Boston Aero Meet, which ran from September 3-13, 1910. Claude Grahame-White's plane is in the center, #3. Courtesy the Library of Congress.

person. Less than seven years after the Wright Brothers ushered in the era of flight at Kitty Hawk, the leading aviators of the world and pioneers of flight—including Wilbur Wright—gathered in Boston for only the second aviation exhibition ever held on American soil.

The meet was held at an airfield on Squantum Point across from Thompson Island. For nearly two weeks, more than one million people watched in absolute awe at the sight of these strange flying machines and the skill of the daring "bird men." Aviators vied for more than $40,000 in prize money in competitions for speed, altitude, duration, distance, landing, and even for accuracy in dropping fake bombs onto a dummy battleship. The most anticipated event, however, was the $10,000 prize put up by *The Boston Globe* for the fastest time in completing two nonstop laps from the airfield around Boston Light, a distance of thirty-three miles.

Famed English aviator Claude Grahame-White stole the show. The crowd was electric when Grahame-White, dressed in a brown canvas aviation suit, donned his head gear, adjusted his ear flaps, and mounted his machine in an attempt to make history. The engine of his monoplane hummed as he made his way down the runway and lifted off the ground, fading into the distance until he became a mere speck against the blue sky. Tens of thousands of people lined the hillsides and roofs of Hull, while passengers on a veritable fleet of boats in the harbor kept their eyes to the sky. Grahame-White passed so low over the harbor islands that it is said he scared the chickens kept on Peddocks. He then made the first of two great, wide curves around Little Brewster's tower and another lap before he returned to the airfield where he was greeted by the wild cheers of thousands in the grandstand and the honking horns of those watching from their automobiles. *The Boston Globe* called it the "first great race by a birdman ever seen in this part of the world." Grahame-White would complete the route a second time, and he would be the only competitor to complete the flight over Boston Light.

Two decades after the pioneers of flight whizzed above the head of the keeper of Boston Light, another winged visitor—the stork—dropped by Little Brewster Island. A doctor and a Coast Guard crew braved a Nor'easter and blinding rain in the middle of the night to travel from Hull to the island to assist in the delivery of assistant keeper Ralph Norwood's seventh child, Georgia. (Two weeks prior, they faced an even fiercer storm in making the journey only to discover it was a false alarm!) The story inspired Ruth Carmen to write the novel *Storm Child*. When Georgia was five years old, she was slated to play herself in a movie version of the story. In the end, the family chose to eschew Hollywood stardom to stay at Boston Light, and the movie fell through.

At one point in the 1930s, the population of Little Brewster Island exploded to more than three keepers, their wives, and nineteen children. Sixty years later, it appeared that the island population would shrink to zero as the automation of lighthouses across the country appeared to render the keeper position obsolete. In actuality, Boston Light was the last lighthouse in the U.S. to be automated in 1998, and even then, preservation groups successfully appealed to retain a human presence on Little Brewster. To this day, Boston Light is the only remaining Coast Guard lighthouse with an official keeper.

In 2003, Sally Snowman was installed as the seventieth keeper of Boston Light—and the first female to ever hold the position. With the help of assistant light keepers and volunteers, Sally continues many of the rituals of her sixty-nine predecessors, such as inspecting the lighthouse lens, polishing its grass prisms, logging meteorological data, and maintaining the island's buildings. Unlike early guardians of the light, however, she also conducts seasonal tours and develops educational programs.

More than 3,700 people visit the island each year, with 2,500 climbing to the top of the lighthouse. Massive iron doors at the base of the lighthouse, bearing the imprint of the South Boston Iron Company, open into the tower. A spiral staircase of seventy-six steps and two short ladders lead to the top of the lighthouse. Those who scale the tower come face-to-face with

Little Brewster Island Circa 1906. Courtesy the Library of Congress, Detroit Publishing Company Collection.

the giant 4,000-pound Fresnel lens, nine feet tall and dotted with 336 twelve-sided glass prisms that resemble a kaleidoscope. The Coast Guard has just completed the first full preservation of the lens since it was installed in 1859. The view from the top of the lighthouse is a magnificent panorama of the harbor, its islands, the open Atlantic, and the Boston skyline nearly ten miles away.

A small vestibule at the base of the lighthouse functions as a museum that includes lighthouse artifacts and early navigation aids. The most prized possession—and the Coast Guard's oldest artifact—is the station's fog cannon that dates back to 1719. Keepers would fire the cannon to answer blasts from ships that found themselves blanketed in by the fog. A fog bell replaced the cannon in 1851, and a siren was added in the 1880s. A bell similar to the one used at Boston Light stands outside the entrance to the lighthouse tower.

In addition to the lighthouse tower, there are five other whitewashed structures on Little Brewster Island, including an engine house, boathouse, cistern building, and oil house, all which date from the nineteenth century. Perched on top of the rocky ledges, these gable-roofed buildings give the appearance of a tiny New England fishing village. There are no shrubs or trees, and most of the island is covered by a green lawn and colorful wildflowers in the summer and early fall. Cormorants and gulls roost on the island's rocky ledges and fish the nearby waters.

The keeper's house, with an American flag proudly flying in front, dates from 1884. The two-story house has high ceilings, hardwood floors, and large windows that let in the light. This white clapboard house could be just about any old New England home—except for the venerable lighthouse that continues to stand watch right outside its door.

Sally Snowman, the 70th keeper of Boston Light, greets visitors in 18th century dress.

The Coast Guard has just completed the first full preservation of the Fresnel lens since it was installed in 1859.

ADDITIONAL INFORMATION

Ranger-guided tours of Little Brewster Island and Boston Light are available between June and September. Tours run Friday through Sunday. The three-hour trip includes a narrated tour of Boston Harbor and a chance to scale Boston Light. Ferries depart from the Fort Point Channel side of the Moakley United States Courthouse at Fan Pier in the South Boston Seaport District. Children must be eight years old or fifty inches tall to climb the lighthouse. To purchase tickets or for more information, visit www.harborislands.org or call 617-223-8666. At the time of publication, ferry tickets cost $39 for adults, $35 for seniors, and $29 for youth between the ages of three and eleven.

Between June and September, Little Brewster Island is open to private boaters on Fridays, Saturdays, and Sundays between 12:30 PM and 3:00 PM for drop-off and pick-up only. There is no docking at Little Brewster Island, and boats must anchor offshore.

Great Brewster Island

The massive escarpment of Great Brewster Island is one of the most recognizable landmarks in Boston Harbor. The island's northern bluff, weather-beaten and scarred from thousands of years of the ocean's abuse, has eroded into a sheer cliff of sand. For generations of Boston mariners, the northern bluff of Great Brewster Island has been a welcome sign that they were nearly home. For boats leaving the Boston waterfront, it's a familiar pointer toward open waters.

At over one hundred feet high, the bluff on Great Brewster is striking even from miles away. That it becomes even more awe-inspiring as you navigate along its shoreline is one of Mother Nature's pleasant tricks. Looking up at the cliff from the surface of the harbor, it feels as if you are at the bottom of a canyon and a giant claw has taken a swipe at the island's side. Whole sections of the bluff have been lost to landslides and washed away with the tide. The ridges that have formed along the side of the cliff offer a lovely interplay of light and shadows changing as the sun moves across the sky, with the most picturesque colors emerging at sunset. The view is just as scenic when you alight onto the island and scale the summit of its northern bluff, the highest

point in the outer harbor. It can be a bit of a workout, but the payoff is worth it. The water of the outer harbor sparkles, and if you listen closely, you can hear the cries of the cormorants on nearby Shag Rocks.

As the largest of those in the outer harbor, Great Brewster is filled with both natural and man-made wonders that can entertain for hours. Hiking trails and mowed paths make it easy to wander across the island, and numerous picnic tables provide plenty of opportunities to relax and enjoy the surroundings. Unfortunately, the dock has been washed away, so there is no longer public ferry service to the island. Do not let this deter you; kayaks and flat-bottomed boats can land on the island's western beach, and staging a beach landing is well worth it.

The Brewsters (Great Brewster, Little Brewster, Middle Brewster, and Outer Brewster Islands) are said to be named in honor of Elder William Brewster, the spiritual leader of the Pilgrims. Brewster, the first preacher and teacher of the Plymouth Bay Colony, played a major role in planning and organizing the voyage of the *Mayflower* to America.

Naming these islands after a Pilgrim who sought safe harbor in America is apt, since the Brewsters ensure the safety of Boston Harbor. These rugged, windswept islands form a natural breakwater, shielding the inner harbor from the wrath of the open ocean. The other islands in the Brewster chain are outcroppings of bedrock, giving them the strength to weather such wicked conditions. Great Brewster, however, is a drumlin island created by glacial deposits of clay and gravel, and that softer geological composition makes it more vulnerable to erosion. Completely exposed to easterly gales, the island has borne the brunt of nature's fury for thousands of years.

By the middle of the nineteenth century, eroded material from the island began to fill up the shipping channel and posed a considerable threat to commerce. As a result, the federal government in 1848 began construction of a massive seawall to protect the island and the channel. The enormous granite blocks of the seawall around the north and south heads and along the eastern shore of Great Brewster Island remain today. Sections of the seawall are still intact, but decades of ravaging waves have taken their toll and some portions are now in disrepair. Be sure to heed the "No Trespassing" signs where they are posted.

In some sections, the mighty sea has smashed through the gray slabs of granite as if they were mere building blocks. Crumbled stretches of the seawall have given birth to thriving tidal pools among the rocks. The tidal pools support mussels, snails, starfish, and crabs as well as lichens and barnacles. This convenient supply of food sustains a colony of gulls on the island. It's a common sight to look above and see the skies filled with gulls, their wings spread as they glide through the air. The east side of the island, along the seawall, is a breeding ground in the early summer for Herring (gray-winged) and Great Black-backed (black-winged) Gulls. Young gulls usually hatch in June and take flight by August. Gulls are very protective of their young during nesting and rearing season and might swoop aggressively to scare unwanted intruders away, so it's wise to keep your distance at those times of the year.

The middle portion of Great Brewster Island is dominated by a salt marsh, which can be inundated in stormy weather and during the winter, but dries up in the summer months. This area of the island is relatively devoid of sumac groves and trees, which allows for a fantastic, unencumbered panorama of Boston Harbor. Looking west, the skyscrapers of downtown Boston and the egg digesters of Deer Island rise above the grasses and cattails growing in the marsh. Turning to the east, the stately white pillar of Boston Light, less than a half mile away, soars above the seawall. Shutterbugs will be pleased by the exceptional snapshots they'll be able to get from this vantage point.

With Great Brewster and Little Brewster Islands separated by only a shallow sandbar, the keepers of Boston Light often traveled to Great Brewster. George Worthylake, the first keeper of Boston Light, is said to have grazed sheep on Great Brewster, and for many years, a well on the island supplied keepers of Boston Light with drinking water. During the 1700s and 1800s, in addition to grazing livestock, Great Brewster Island was used to supply stone and gravel ballast for thousands of ships, which no doubt helped contribute to its wearing away.

By the latter half of the nineteenth century, Great Brewster Island became home to a handful of summer residents. Benjamin Dean, who owned Outer Brewster Island and was a member of the U.S. House of Representatives, moved his summer villa to the island sometime around 1875. The island was also a seasonal home for fishermen, and by the 1930s, about a dozen families had summer cottages on the island. Sporadic stone wall foundations and remnants of plants cultivated by residents, such as asparagus and Concord grapes, can still be spotted on the island.

The cottage community came to an end with the outbreak of World War II. To help protect the city, the federal government took over the island, which held strategic importance at the entrance to Boston Harbor. The Army deployed 120 soldiers from Fort Strong on Long Island to Great Brewster Island, and the new military reservation included a mess hall, barracks, post exchange, and pump house.

The military placed a battery of 90-millimeter rapid-fire guns on the northern bluff to ward off torpedo boats. It also stationed anti-aircraft guns, observation posts, and searchlights on the island, but Great Brewster's primary use was as a command post that assisted in controlling the electronically operated minefields in Boston Harbor. A bomb- and gas-proof bunker, burrowed into the island's south hill, was filled with electronic equipment to assist Fort Dawes on Deer Island with the operation of mines along the north channel of Boston Harbor. Signals were transmitted from an observation constructed on top.

Unfortunately, World War II was not the first time that Great Brewster Island was touched by armed conflict. Massachusetts General Court records indicate that Great Brewster Island was used as an internment site for Native Americans during King Philip's War. A November 1675 order directed Native American women who chose not to join their husbands in prison or on Deer Island be sent to Great Brewster Island. A few months later, the General Court compensated colonists who owned the island for its use in confining the Native Americans.

Many of the military buildings built during World War II were removed after its conclusion, but some concrete foundations of the buildings and platforms for the searchlights and gun batteries can still be seen today. The shell of the bunker in the south hill also remains, but there is little to see other than its bare concrete walls. Exploration is unadvisable as it is dark and contains asbestos. What's much more enjoyable is a walk along the sweeping, rocky beaches below the entrance to the bunker.

Walking south along the beach leads to the Great Brewster Spit, extending from the southwestern tip of the island. The spit is exposed at low tide, and though it may look inviting for the adventurous explorer, tidal currents and slippery rocks can make it extremely dangerous.

The arched breakwater snakes for nearly a mile before it ends near Lovells Island at the entrance to the Narrows Channel, once the main shipping route to Boston. For more than seventy years, an odd-looking red lighthouse stood guard at the end of the bar as a warning to mariners of the hidden danger. The Narrows Light, erected in 1856, was in reality a dwelling with its roof cut to allow its warning beacon to be seen. The wooden, hexagonal structure was perched thirty-five feet high above the sea on seven spindly iron stilts, which gave it the appearance of a huge water insect and earned it the endearing nickname of "Bug Light."

On the morning of June 7, 1929, keeper Thomas Small was using a blowtorch to remove paint from the outside walls of Bug Light when suddenly a portion of the wall above his head caught fire. The flames were fed by the winds and overtook the lighthouse in just minutes. Small barely escaped before Bug Light collapsed into the harbor, launching seaspray high into the air. All that remained was a twisted mess of iron.

After wandering the rugged terrain of Great Brewster, you'll no doubt be hungry. A set of picnic tables on the crest of the island's southern hill above the spit is the perfect place for a picnic. Face one way toward the city or face the other toward Boston Light. It's a setting that captures the essence of the outer harbor islands: an extraordinary ocean wilderness teetering between the open waters to the east and the bustling city to the west.

Photographing the Harbor Islands

Sherman "Pat" Morss, Jr., is one of the original members of the Boston Harbor Islands Advisory Council and the photographer of Boston Harbor Islands, *which draws from a collection of 1,800 photographs and his intimate knowledge of the harbor islands.*

"Most people access the Boston Harbor Islands by ferry, from the mainland to Spectacle or Georges Island. Spectacle has stunning harbor views and close-ups of a newly planted ecosystem. You can spend a day photographing the spooky sanctums of star-shaped Fort Warren on Georges Island.

"The light on both islands will be best if you take the earliest ferry or stay for sunset. In between, take the shuttle from either hub to one of the other islands served. Peddocks has great diversity with historic Fort Andrews to the north, the park's only private cottage community in the center, and

a nature preserve to the south. Spend a night camping on Grape or Bumpkin Island for more extensive photo opportunities. And don't miss the separate ferry trips directly to Little Brewster, where you can climb Boston Light.

"A private boat or kayak broadens the photographic possibilities. The islands of Hingham Bay are rarely visited and are sheltered for small craft. Venture further out into Massachusetts Bay if the forecast is for safe conditions. Except for Little Brewster, these are remote sanctuaries for birds and forgotten fortifications.

"Don't stay home in the off season. Visit the 'mainland islands.' Cross country ski around the stark white, other-worldly sewage digesters on Deer Island. Walk through the fall foliage at World's End.

"Having experienced the diversity of all the islands, it is difficult to say which is

my favorite for photographs. But I do have a favorite experience. I asked Sally Snowman, light keeper at Boston Light, whether I might stay past the tourist departure to photograph sunset from the lighthouse. To my astonishment she suggested I spend the night in the keeper's house. On the appointed afternoon she handed me a flashlight, an emergency radio, and the key to the lighthouse tower. Sunset over Boston and its harbor was magnificent. But the remoteness after dark—when the planes stopped flying, the city lights receded, and the pinwheel of six lights from the Fresnel lenses revolved overhead—was extraordinary. I was back up to the lantern level before dawn to witness sunrise over the Atlantic, focusing my thoughts on a greater world than the man-made city of the previous evening's sunset."

For more information about Pat's photography, visit: www.morssphoto.com.

Middle Brewster Island

No American city has stronger Irish roots than Boston, and no landscape in metropolitan Boston is more evocative of the Emerald Isle than Middle Brewster Island. The cliffs, the pounding Atlantic surf, the stone walls, and the crumbling ruins strewn across a field of windswept grass offers the same blend of raw and rugged wilderness that lures so many to Ireland's romantic shores.

In the center of this wild and untamed landscape is an old arch, standing ten feet high. When viewed from just the right perspective, the lichen-coated archway perfectly frames the distant Boston skyline. Once the entrance to the white brick villa that commanded a cliff on the island's southwest corner, the arch is little more than a relic from a time when Middle Brewster was a summer retreat for some of Boston's most prominent citizens.

The first of these notable Bostonians who spent their summers on Middle Brewster Island was Augustus Russ, the founder of the Boston Yacht Club and one of the city's best-known lawyers. Russ purchased the island in 1871 and leased several lots to other residents, including millionaire Benjamin P. Cheney and his wife, Julia Arthur. Before the couple built their palatial estate on neighboring Calf Island, they lived on Middle Brewster in a more modest home, "The Capstan."

This photo, from The New England Magazine *of October 1895, shows the summer community that once occupied the island. Courtesy Anthony Sammarco.*

Russ enjoyed spending his summer days and nights in solitude on Middle Brewster while commuting daily to and from Boston in his yacht. After Russ passed away in 1892, the island was purchased by one of his law partners, Melvin O. Adams. One of the most-celebrated lawyers in Massachusetts, Adams served as an assistant district attorney in Suffolk County, a district attorney for the federal government, and also president of the Boston, Revere Beach & Lynn Railroad. His great fame, however, came from his role on the defense team during the 1893 trial of the infamous Lizzie Borden, who was accused and acquitted of hacking her father and stepmother to death with an axe. One paper of the time described Adams as "the eyes, the ears, and the directing hand of the defense."

Sharing the island with these Gilded Age figures was a colony of fishermen and their families, who began living on Middle Brewster Island in the middle of the nineteenth century. One of these humble cottages was the scene of a very bizarre—and tragic—fatality in 1923. On a June morning, Victor Ciarmataro joined his father and brother on a motorboat trip from their home in the North End to the Brewsters to

Following his time in the service and before becoming dockmaster at Hingham Shipyard Marinas, Chuck Zonderman was a commercial lobsterman for thirty years. When he wasn't working, he was pleasure boating — few people are as knowledgeable as he about fishing Boston Harbor.

"When it comes to fishing, knowing the types of water different fish like is half the battle. Using the correct bait accounts for most of the other half.

"Early fall is the time to go bass fishing, though they're around as early as April. Flocks of birds feeding on bait fish are a good indication they're around. Look around river mouths for early bass. (Try the Back River and the Fore River.) Bigger bass come into the harbor in search of the warm water found in the deeper channels. A popular rig to use is a tube and worm, though last season the fishermen's preference was for live bait fish. Chunking works well, too. Anchor your boat and let the bait drift down tide.

"These days, codfish are not as prevalent in the spring, though we'll see them later into the fall. You'll find rock cod around Point Allerton and Boston Light, and larger ocean cod around the B-buoy, Thieves Ledge off Hull, and Graves and Minot's Light. Cod prefer clams to sea worms. A weighted lure with a treble hook, or a cod jig works well.

"In the late fall, the flounder start showing up. Flounder are soft-bottom fish. They dig in the mud for the winter. By early December, they're pretty much dormant. Try around Peddocks, Rainsford, Long, and Green Islands—or anywhere there's soft bottom, even in shallow water. Flounder return in the spring, when the water starts to warm. By mid-summer, they're only

For current fishing regulations visit, www.nero.noaa.gov.

found offshore. They're great eating fish and sea worms tend to be the best bait.

"Bluefish are a warmer water fish then cod. They come through in the early summer, chasing poagies in a frenzy. Like mackerel, bluefish can be caught while they are feeding near the surface of the water. Blues (and big bass) are also out in the deeper water around the B-buoy, and can be caught both on the surface and deeper down. Bluefish and bass are readily caught as far in as Wollaston Beach. Good spots for mackerel are Harding's Ledge off of Nantasket, the Bay off Pemberton, and A Street in Hull on the bayside.

"We used to see haddock around Graves Light, but these days you have to go further into open water. There's some small tuna fishing offshore. Occasionally you'll see them around Minot's Ledge or inside the B-buoy. (You'll also see whales and dolphin just to the east of these offshore ledges.) Outside the Brewster Islands, you might find some good size sharks, too."

Chuck Zonderman

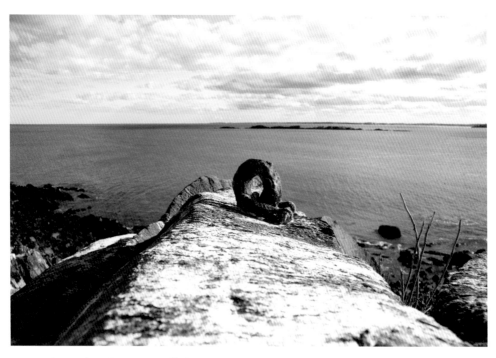

The view from the southern cliff of Middle Brewster. Shag Rocks in the distance.

harvest periwinkles. After a few hours of work, the teenage boy was thirsty, so he knocked on the door of the home of the island's caretaker, Hjalmar Roos, for a drink. Getting no answer, the boy went around to the window on the back porch and found that it was unlocked.

Victor decided to open the window, which, unfortunately, proved to be a deadly decision. Roos, plagued by thefts while he was out fishing, had booby trapped the window so that a rifle would fire. As soon as Victor pushed up the sash, he was shot in the stomach. The caretaker pled guilty to manslaughter, but he was only fined $750 since the boy was ruled to have been breaking and entering. Eight years later, Roos was ordered to pay civil damages of $6,000. The descendants of Melvin Adams paid both fines, and Roos continued to live on the island, serving as its caretaker.

These days, birds are the primary residents of Middle Brewster Island, and a small freshwater marsh on the eastern side attracts a wide variety. Rookeries for two species of herons are found on the island's southeast corner, and it is a nesting site for gulls and cormorants. Visitation is greatly discouraged during nesting time.

Middle Brewster is an untamed ocean wilderness, and even for the most experienced adventurer, exploring this island can be dangerous. Access is understandably (though regrettably) discouraged. The cliffs, nearly perpendicular in spots, and the sunken crags that surround the island make it rather complicated to get ashore. And there are few beaches and inlets on which to land, making it the most inaccessible of the Brewsters. The interior of the island is equally challenging to navigate. There are no trails to follow, and thickets are a constant impediment.

Still, Middle Brewster is possibly the most beautiful and romantic island in Boston Harbor—in no small part because of the house foundations, crumbling fireplaces, and stone walls that once demarcated the island's properties. Though they are now weathered and overgrown, these ruins provide mystical clues as to how this terrain once looked when the summer colony thrived. And, of course, there is the arch. Luckily, it is just as lovely from the water.

Outer Brewster Island

From the weather-beaten cliffs on the eastern side of Outer Brewster Island all that separates you from Spain is three thousand miles of open ocean.

As the easternmost island in the park, remote Outer Brewster is also the most threatened by human activity. It began when Nathaniel Austin Jr., Middlesex County sheriff and state senator, quarried rock from the island's shores for the city's buildings and street pavement. In the 1820s, stone removed from Outer Brewster was used to construct the three-story Austin Block, which still stands at 92 Main Street in Charlestown near the historic Warren Tavern. When the Austin Block was renovated in the 1980s, stone was again harvested from Outer Brewster to restore the first floor. Outer Brewster's stone also paved the Warren Bridge, which connected Charlestown to the North End. (Law students might recall the construction of the bridge led to the famous 1837 case *Charles River Bridge v. Warren Bridge* that was argued before the U.S. Supreme Court.)

According to some historical accounts, Nathaniel Austin's brother, Arthur, who was deeded the island in the 1840s, attempted to cut a narrow channel through the island's solid rock so that boats could find refuge in stormy weather. A lengthy canal was excavated, but this particular "big dig" was never completed. The channel, which nearly divides the island in two, remains today.

During the nineteenth century, Bostonians took advantage of Outer Brewster Island's seclusion to engage in activities that were frowned upon within the city limits, such as illegal boxing matches. One such bout, which the *Boston Democrat* referred to as "one of these disgusting and brutal exhibitions," occurred in 1844. Under the cover of darkness, pugilists Joe Long and an Englishman named Smith—along with two hundred spectators—set sail from Boston at two o'clock in the morning. When the fight finally began at nine o'clock, it lasted two hours and one hundred rounds before Long emerged victorious. The *Boston Democrat* was outraged and hoped "the parties to this most disgraceful affair" would be appropriately punished.

Outer Brewster's relatively barren landscape and rocky shoreline made the island essentially uninhabitable, although a small group of fishermen and lobstermen did reside there in the latter half of the nineteenth century. By the time the federal government purchased the island in 1913 (for a mere $2,500), there was just a single fisherman living on its shores.

The government bought the island in the name of coastal defense, but it wasn't fortified until 1942, after the outbreak of World War II. The Outer Brewster Military Reservation included a 6-inch shielded gun emplacement, three barracks capable of housing 125 men, a mess hall, a desalinization plant, and a long-range radar unit mounted on a 100-foot tower.

Today, the ruins of the military reservation, deactivated after World War II, are prominent on the middle and western end of the island. The gray concrete shells of the barracks, now surrounded by a maze of sumac, occupy the island's western bluffs. Surely, there were few soldiers during the war who had a better view than the ones who lived in the barracks on Outer Brewster.

The circular gun batteries, the base of the radar tower, and the entrance to Battery

Jewell are impossible to miss. Built beneath the island's highest crest, the battery served as a bomb- and chemical-proof bunker. Entering the tunnels and abandoned ammunition rooms inside the battery and barracks are discouraged, and generally visitors should take care to avoid any unmarked and uncovered wells and pits that remain from the island's military days.

Left: Arthur Austin's unfinished channel nearly divided Outer Brewster into two islands.

Some well-trodden paths on parts of the island make it easier to hike Outer Brewster than the other islands in the outer harbor, but the high bluffs and rocky shoreline make Outer Brewster equally difficult to access. During rough weather, the island is virtually unapproachable.

If the tide is right, however, a small rocky cove on the island's northern shore offers a good spot for dinghies or kayaks to come ashore. To the east of the cove is the fissure that remains from Arthur Austin's abandoned plans to build an artificial harbor. Even if the channel is dry, some rock scaling is required to cross to the island's eastern end.

Just to the west of the cove, along the island's northern shore, is the island's most unique natural geological form—Pulpit Rock, named for its resemblance to a minister's podium. When the wind blows across this tall, table-top formation it sounds as if Mother Nature herself is shaking the rock, ferociously declaring her almighty power.

Since Outer Brewster Island is so windswept and exposed to the elements, only a small stand of quaking aspens can be found. Much of the island is covered with tall grass and staghorn sumac, which is thickest around the military ruins. What the island lacks in flora it makes up for in fauna, and Outer Brewster supports one of the most diverse collections of breeding water birds in Boston Harbor. The island provides a nesting habitat for coastal waterbirds such as cormorants, wading birds, waterfowl, shorebirds, and gulls. American Oystercatchers and Common Eider nest on the island, and ibis have been spotted as well. As birds can be aggressive during nesting season, access is discouraged at that time.

The cleanup of Boston Harbor has revitalized the aquatic wildlife around Outer Brewster Island as well. By the 1980s, pollution made the harbor devoid of the biodiversity that attracts large marine animals, such as seals and porpoises. Now that smelt, herring, and mackerel populations have rebounded, the seals and porpoises have returned. White and brown seals can be seen on the rocks of Outer Brewster

The Boston Harbor Islands is considered an Important Bird Area by organizations such as the Massachusetts Audubon Society. A variety of habitats (marine, rock cliff, beach, salt marsh, and forest) support over one hundred species.

Many species of waterbirds nest on the islands. It is common to see large colonies of Double-crested Cormorants, Herring Gulls, Great Black-backed Gulls, and Common Eiders on the rocky shores and scrub habitats of the outer islands. A colony of Least Terns, a state listed species, occurs on Rainsford Island.

Black-crowned Night-Herons, Snowy Egrets, Great Egrets, and to a lesser extent, Glossy Ibis, breed among the islands, as well. These wading birds nest in the trees along the coast-lines. Sarah Island has the largest wading bird colony in the harbor. Recently, American Oystercatchers were recorded on Slate, Lovells, and Snake Islands.

As suspected, smaller islands have less diverse populations of breeding landbirds than larger islands. It is believed that Peddocks Island has as many as thirty-four breeding species. Landbirds such as Song Sparrows, Red-winged Blackbirds, and Yellow Warblers are common to the area. The more widespread Savannah Sparrow can be found nesting on the restored grasslands of Spectacle Island.

Migrating shorebirds are most commonly found on Snake, Rainsford, and Great Brewster Islands from July through August. In the past, sightings have included Black-bellied Plovers, Purple Sandpipers, and Ruddy Turnstones.

Park managers use the size of the breeding bird populations and the number of nests, eggs, and chicks to gauge the environmental health of the park. Breeding season occurs from May through the end of July. The public is asked to respect this delicate stage in the life cycle and not to disturb the colonies while they are at work.

Bird lovers should check out eBird, a database for birdwatchers. Contributing your observations will help scientists understand species distribution and movement patterns in Massachusetts and across the continent. www.ebird.org

Top: Ruddy Turnstone, Purple Sandpiper, female Eider. Bottom: Snowy Egret, Lesser Yellowlegs, Piping Plover.

and the nearby islands, more so in the wintertime. Also thanks to the harbor cleanup, the water around Outer Brewster offers the best scuba diving around Boston.

Arthur Austin's designs for an artificial harbor may have left a permanent scar on Outer Brewster, but other development plans hatched over the years could have obliterated the island's landscape altogether. In the 1960s and 1970s, propositions to fill in the harbor between the Brewsters to build a trash dump, recreation area, and even an airport were considered. Most recently, AES Corporation, one of the world's largest power companies, proposed construction of a $500 million import and storage facility for liquefied natural gas (LNG) on Outer Brewster. The proposal called for blasting out the interior of the island to build two 100-foot-deep tanks and restricting access to fishing and boating around the island. Massachusetts owns Outer Brewster Island, and despite its incorporation into the Boston Harbor Islands national park area in 1996, the state retains the right to sell it to a private interest. Amazingly, the LNG proposal found backers in the state legislature. Thankfully, after an intense two-year fight by a coalition of environmental organizations and island lovers, the proposal lacked sufficient legislative support to be enacted. However, it stands as a distressing example of the threat that continues to faces the Boston Harbor Islands—and, in particular, this most remote of isles.

Calf Island

The red brick chimney towering over the landscape of Calf Island stands testament to a bygone era when the islands served as personal retreats for some of Boston's wealthiest residents. Today, sumacs sprout from the foundation that once supported the palatial summer home of millionaire railroad financier Benjamin P. Cheney, Jr. and the beautiful Shakespearean stage actress Julia Arthur. Built in 1902 after the couple moved from Middle Brewster, their estate, "The Moorings," would have been equally at home among the mansions of Newport.

The Moorings dominated the crest of Calf Island, facing west toward Boston and commanding a broad sweep of the sea on all sides. *The Boston Globe* described it as the "first beauty touch to be given to one of the gaunt, inhospitable-looking Brewster islands." The two-story home was gigantic—twenty rooms in all—and lavishly decorated. The furniture was made of solid oak, the ceilings and floors were made of hard pine, and photographs and paintings adorned the exquisite cypress-paneled walls. Outside, a stone veranda ran along three sides of the house.

With a half-dozen guest rooms, the Cheneys were constantly entertaining. Their guests must have spent hours soaking in the glorious panorama from the stone belvedere built on the precipitous cliff in front of the house, below which Benjamin

Cheney docked his steam launch and yacht. Eight servants were needed to tend to the property, and a large boathouse included their sleeping and living quarters.

The Cheneys planned to add a swimming pool and golf links to the estate, but those plans never came to fruition, and the couple's carefree days on Calf Island came to an abrupt end in a stunning reversal of fortune. In 1917, Cheney, who had inherited $10 million, shocked the city by declaring bankruptcy. Three years later, the treasures of The Moorings were picked over by prospective buyers at auction. Julia Arthur, who had vowed never to act again when she moved to Calf Island, was forced to return to the stage.

The government ended up seizing Calf Island and The Moorings by eminent domain for military use at the onset of World War I, and over the decades the estate fell victim to fire and vandals. (Cheney himself met a strange death in 1942, when he apparently died of dehydration in an Arizona desert—an ironic end for a man who spent glorious summers at the water's edge.)

It seems Calf Island was always fit for kings and queens. Decades before the Cheneys arrived, a small colony of lobstermen and fishermen lived on Calf Island. Their humble cottages couldn't have been more different from The Moorings—and no Calf Island resident was more salty or eccentric than James J. Turner, the anointed "King of Calf Island."

Turner, a lobsterman, moved to Calf Island in the 1840s and lived there for nearly forty years until he passed away at ninety. He was a wild and unkempt man, and an illustration of Turner in his later years depicts him as weather-beaten and gaunt, with a long white beard hiding his face. Rumors swirled that the King had been a pirate and murderer in a previous life.

Julia Arthur, queen of the stage, vowed never to act again once she and her husband moved to Calf Island from Middle Brewster. Courtesy the Library of Congress.

The "palace" from which the King of Calf Island reigned was a modest cottage that included the chartroom and pilot house from the wrecked steamer *Ontario*, which Turner had towed over from Apple Island. He lived in the cottage with his son, James E. Turner, who was six years old when his father brought him to Calf Island. The elder Turner, a strict disciplinarian, forced his son to perform military drills with a rifle for hours on end. On Sundays, the King would review the drills while dressed in a Turkish outfit that included a red sash and fez. Despite this strange upbringing, James E. Turner developed an affinity for Calf Island, too. He lived there for more than fifty years, and in true dynastic succession, the son became known as the "Emperor of Calf Island."

The fishermen who lived on the island, including the Turners, courageously rescued shipwreck survivors and buried the victims in unmarked graves at the top of the island. According to historical accounts, the primitive graveyard contains the remains of twenty-one sailors lost in nearby waters. The conditions around Calf Island were so treacherous that the Massachusetts Humane Society built one of its first huts of refuge on its southwest coast in 1789.

Calf Island has seen a wide range of uses over the centuries. There is evidence that Native Americans occupied the island seasonally, and the island was used to pasture livestock by early European settlers. In the late nineteenth century, Bostonians spent summer Sundays recreating on the island, and there were frequent reports of illicit boxing matches on the Sabbath. While the federal government acquired the rights to Calf Island in 1917, it didn't see much military activity until World War II, when it was home to a small garrison that manned an advanced anti-aircraft searchlight, radar, and observation site.

Today, there are no remains of the military reservation and little signs of previous human activity other than the ruins of The Moorings

The view toward Outer Brewster.

and a few cultivars, such as cherry trees and mock orange shrubs. The majority of Calf Island is covered by grasses, sumacs, and some salt-tolerant trees.

Calf Island has several beaches where visitors can come ashore in a dinghy or kayak. One of the better landing spots is in a sandy cove on the island's western shore. If the water is too rough on the west side of the island, a rocky but protected beach on the island's east side offers another option. Several unimproved trails run along the west shore of Calf Island leading to the ruins of The Moorings, but overall the island is difficult to traverse. At its center is a freshwater pond surrounded by tidal marshes.

Most visitors to Calf Island are drawn to the ruins of Benjamin P. Cheney's house and that lone chimney—the last of the estate's five great fireplaces. Julia Arthur's

monogram was inlaid in the dining room fireplace, which is now gone. The remaining chimney, which heated the billiards room, still boasts Cheney's initials, "BP," fashioned from white sea pebbles. All it takes is a little imagination to feel the hardwood floors beneath your feet, see the summer breeze ruffling the drapes, and hear the voice of old B.P. telling you to "Rack 'em!"

At the island's center is a freshwater pond.

Little Calf Island

Little Calf Island is just over one hundred yards north of its big brother, Calf Island. At low tide the two islands might seem as though they are connected, and at one time they probably were. The shallow passage between is rife with hidden ledges and shoals. Mariners should take extreme caution if they attempt to pass between the islands.

Little Calf Island is tiny, desolate, and devoid of vegetation. In 1835, the owner of Little Calf tried to lease the island on the implausible proposition that it was ideally suited to pasturing sheep or a fishing camp. Even though centuries of Poseidon's fury has likely reduced the island to its diminutive size — Little Calf weighs in at less than an acre — these selling points were for the birds. Literally.

The island is a nesting site for Herring Gulls, Black-backed Gulls, and cormorants. It's not unusual to find hundreds of birds perched on the surf-beaten rocks. Alas, even if you did want to explore this rugged landscape, there is no safe place to land. Luckily, the on-water views are just as good.

Green Island

North of Little Calf Island is rocky Green Island, the two islands separated by the swift-flowing waters of Hypocrite Channel. On early maps, Green Island was labeled as "North Brewster Island." According to some historical accounts of the islands, Green Island received its current name from Joseph Green, a colonial Boston merchant, said to have owned the island at one time.

The islands in Boston Harbor certainly attracted their fair share of nonconformists and Green Island was no exception. It was home to the recluse Samuel Choate, who built a rudimentary hut made of driftwood in 1845 and lived on the island for twenty years, subsisting on fish, lobster, and the mussels he harvested around the islands. *The Boston Journal* described Choate as a "hermit of somewhat singular habits, and possessing a very independent spirit." (One begs to ask if that isn't true of all hermits.)

Despite the miserable, harsh winters Choate must have endured, he remained on that bleak island until he was nearly seventy years of age, when he was finally induced by the Harbor Police to return to civilization. Shortly after leaving the island, Choate passed away in a Bridgewater almshouse.

Through the 1800s and into the early 1900s, fishermen and lobstermen lived in shanties on Green Island, but there are no traces of this community on the island's nearly two acres today. With little soil and plant life, it is a refuge and nesting spot for gulls, cormorants, and other birds. Beaches are lacking on Green Island, and the rocky ledges surrounding the island make landing difficult and dangerous. Accordingly, public access to Green Island is discouraged.

Shag Rocks

From afar, they appear as tiny little dots on the rocks protruding from the sea, but as you draw closer, the shapes begin to take form, revealing a scene reminiscent of Alfred Hitchcock's movie, *The Birds*. Dozens of cormorants and gulls roost on the bedrock ledges of the curiously named Shag Rocks. (The name makes more sense once you know that cormorants were known as "shags" to the British settlers in Boston.)

Although it's less than a half-mile northeast of Boston Light, Shag Rocks has seen its fair share of shipwrecks, and on numerous occasions the keepers of Boston Light launched rescues for vessels that had run aground on the craggy outcropping. The worst of these wrecks, and one of the most tragic marine disasters ever to happen in Boston Harbor, occurred when a great gale rammed the square-rigger *Maritana* into Shag Rocks just after midnight on November 3, 1861. The powerful storm, which drove the tides above the wharves of the Boston waterfront and nearly to the doors of the Custom House, lodged the *Maritana* between two massive rocks. The crew was forced to cut the masts in attempt to save the ship.

Many dark hours passed without salvation. Shortly after dawn broke, so did the mighty ship. It split in two and plunged twenty-six of the passengers and crew, including women and children, to their deaths. Thirteen people clung tenaciously to the rocks until they were rescued by lifesavers from Hull, nearly twelve hours after their ordeal began. The November 5, 1861, edition of the *Boston Journal* reported: "A more complete wreck was never seen...God save us all from a death like this."

Clearly, Shag Rocks can be a perilous place to approach, and access by boat is impractical. However, while they are a menace to boaters, the large crags and boulders scattered for nearly a third of mile across Shag Rocks create a great lobster-diving and fishing spot—a fact the birds have known for years.

The Graves

It's easy to feel sorry for Graves Light. Even though it's taller and more powerful than Boston Light, Graves Light is often lost in the shadows of its older sibling. Every year, tourists flock to Boston Light, lured by its history and quintessential New England setting. Boston Light even has its own keeper. And Graves Light gets none of this attention.

Truth be told, Graves Light is more imposing than welcoming, and when the fog rolls in, the light can appear downright eerie and haunting. (When the producers of the 1948 motion picture *A Portrait of Jennie* needed a forlorn lighthouse for the climax of their film, they chose Graves Light.) Yet, there is an undeniable majesty to this austere, rock-solid structure.

Graves Light is built upon the hazardous ledges of The Graves, a collection of rock outcroppings that appear appropriately named for the number of vessels that have met catastrophe on their jagged edges. However, The Graves, the outermost point of the Boston Harbor Islands national park area, was supposedly named in the 1600s for Thomas Graves, one of the early Puritan settlers who served on John Winthrop's fleet.

In the centuries after the Puritans arrived in Boston, The Graves proved a menace to mariners. An iron bell buoy was placed near The Graves in the 1850s as a naviga-

tion aid. At the turn of the twentieth century, when a northern entrance to Boston Harbor was dredged in order to accommodate deep-draft ships, a lighthouse was built at its entrance to warn of the dangerous ledges. When its beacon was first lit on September 1, 1905, Graves Light was the most powerful lighthouse along the New England coast.

Even after Graves Light was built, there were still a number of shipwrecks in its vicinity, including the wreck of a latter-day Noah's Ark. In the midst of a dense fog on an April morning in 1938, the British freighter *City of Salisbury* was impaled on an unmarked reef, a half mile from The Graves. The ship was bearing some unusual cargo: a floating menagerie of jungle animals, including a dozen pythons, cobras, tropical birds, three hundred monkeys, and three small honey bears. Fortunately, all passengers (human and otherwise) were rescued before the *City of Salisbury* broke in half the following day. (See page 76 for information about diving near the wreck.)

While numerous boats have succumbed to the sea around The Graves, the light-house's mighty blocks of Cape Ann granite, seven-feet thick at the base, are able to withstand the relentless punishment of the open ocean. The light from the 113-foot tall beacon is visible for twenty-four nautical miles. A ladder forty feet high ascends from the base of the lighthouse to its entrance. The first deck of the tower is used for general storage, and the second is used for fog-signaling apparatus. The space above that was used as living quarters for the keeper when Graves Light was a manned station, and it included a kitchen, bedroom, and library on separate decks. The lantern, automated in 1976 and converted to solar power in 2001, emits two white flashes every twelve seconds.

The lighthouse's original granite oil house still stands atop the rocks of The Graves, but the fog signal house was swept away by the "Perfect Storm" of October 1991. Graves Light is not open to the public, and landing on The Graves is discouraged because of the danger posed by the rocks and surf. Graves Light is certainly in need of its share of sightseers, but cast your awe-inspired gaze from the water.

The Wild Turkey Paddlers is an informal group that provides kayak enthusiasts with an opportunity to meet, participate in trips, and learn about the sport. As a charter member of the group, Nelson Pidgeon has spent years paddling Boston Harbor, visiting many of its islands.

"When we plan a trip we always take the weather and conditions into account. Next to lack of experience, the wind is a kayaker's biggest nemesis. If planned for properly, tides, current, and wind can aid you to and from your destination, making the paddling more enjoyable. But Mother Nature can change her mind, and conditions in Boston's outer harbor can go from dead calm to more wind and waves than you'd care to have. The right gear is extremely important. Never go into open water without a personal flotation device. Proper clothing is also necessary. Other essentials include a bilge pump and paddle float, and a spray skirt to limit water entering the cockpit. Also consider a spare paddle, a compass, a chart of the area, and even a GPS and VHF radio in case of emergency. But none of these items will help you if you don't know how to use them.

"I'd have to say my favorite trip is from Windmill Point in Hull out to Graves Light, which includes a bit of island hopping. You pass through Hull Gut, the waterway between Hull and Peddocks Island. The boat traffic, swift current, and chop make for an exhilarating experience. It's good practice to plan your departure and return with the tides as close to slack as possible. The conditions and traffic in the Gut are almost always exaggerated in the afternoon, as are the number of fishing lines.

"The Graves seems so far away when you start, but it's only about 4.5 miles from Windmill Point, and with the Brewsters, and Calf and Green Islands to add interest it seems to take hardly any time at all. The Graves has a dismal and eerie feel, appearing dark and unfriendly but majestic all at the same time. It is protected from intruders by rocky outcroppings that the waves slap around with intimidating effect. If you're lucky, you might see a seal basking in the sun.

"If your goal is to paddle in the outer harbor, start with a at least a 14-foot sea kayak, though 16 feet and above is preferable. Test as many kayaks as you can to see which fits best. Find out about rudders and skegs.

"A plastic or rotomolded 'poly' boat is a good boat to start with. They're less expensive and will take a beating. Once you've gained some experience, think about upgrading to fiberglass or carbon Kevlar.

"My advice to beginners interested in sea kayaking is to do some initial research. Learn the terminology, understand the skills needed and the potential problems you might run into. Take a course at places like Billington Sea Kayak in Plymouth or Charles River Canoe and Kayak in Newton. If you're interested, the Wild Turkeys offers a bi-weekly paddle out of Hingham Harbor. Hingham Harbor is a great place to get your feet wet, so to speak. It's beautiful and protected with lots of islands to paddle around. Bumpkin and Grape Islands are a little further out and a good next step for venturing into more open water. We don't offer formal training, but our sessions are great ways for beginners to learn and practice their skills in calm water with experienced paddlers. Eventually, you'll be able to take those skills into a more exposed ocean environment for a nice little adventure."

For more information, visit www.wtpaddlers.org.

Logan Airport

Inner Harbor

South Boston

Old Harbor

Columbia Point

Dorchester Bay

Thompson I.

Outward Bound
Education Center

Quincy Bay

Quincy

Map not intended for navigation.

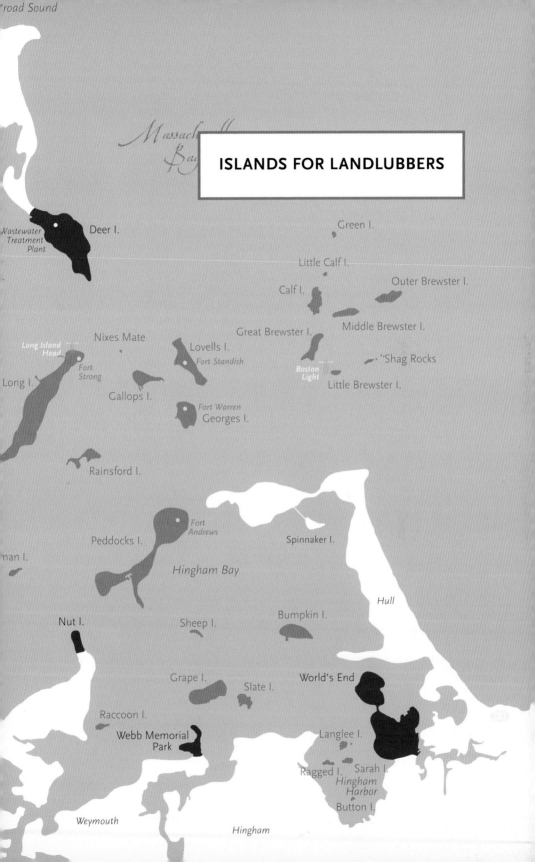

road Sound

Massachusetts Bay

ISLANDS FOR LANDLUBBERS

Wastewater
Treatment
Plant

Deer I.

Green I.

Little Calf I.

Outer Brewster I.

Calf I.

Nixes Mate

Middle Brewster I.

Great Brewster I.

Long Island
Head

Lovells I.
Fort Standish

Fort
Strong

Boston
Light

Shag Rocks

Long I.

Little Brewster I.

Gallops I.

Fort Warren
Georges I.

Rainsford I.

Fort
Andrews

Peddocks I.

Spinnaker I.

man I.

Hingham Bay

Hull

Nut I.

Sheep I.

Bumpkin I.

Grape I.

Slate I.

World's End

Raccoon I.

Langlee I.

Webb Memorial
Park

Ragged I.

Sarah I.

*Hingham
Harbor*

Button I.

Weymouth

Hingham

Deer Island

The twelve egg-shaped structures at the entrance to Boston Harbor often provoke a similar question among first-time visitors: "What the heck are those things?" Well, they are the 130-foot-tall sludge digesters of the massive Deer Island Wastewater Treatment Plant. These funny looking digesters do the dirty, but essential job of breaking down the sludge from wastewater sent to the plant by forty-three communities in metropolitan Boston. Capable of discharging nearly one billion gallons a day, the Deer Island plant sends treated wastewater nearly ten miles offshore through a concrete tunnel, twenty-seven feet in diameter. Without these digesters—and the entire sewage treatment plant that opened in 2001—there wouldn't be a clean harbor, a revitalized waterfront, or even, possibly, a national park area.

The plant is the centerpiece of the $4.5 billion environmental restoration of Boston Harbor that marks the first time Bostonians can point to Deer Island with pride, rather than shame. For centuries, Deer Island was the dismal home of interned Native Americans, quarantined immigrants, orphans, paupers, and criminals. Even today, the voices of those who suffered there seem to whisper in the wind.

Deer Island was a different place when English settlers first arrived in the 1630s. Deer were known to swim across the narrow Shirley Gut that once separated the island from the mainland. (Since the 1930s, when Shirley Gut was filled with sand, Deer Island has been a peninsula connected to the mainland at Winthrop.) The island was heavily wooded, dotted with freshwater ponds, and surrounded by tall bluffs on three sides. As the settlers harvested the island's timber to build their colony, this natural beauty was quickly transformed. Forty years later it would be shattered entirely.

Just over a half-century after the Pilgrims sat down to the first Thanksgiving with the Wampanoag Indians and their great sachem, Massasoit, in 1621, an uneasy peace between the encroaching colonists and Native Americans gave way to a bloody war. Led by Massasoit's son, Metacom, who was known to the English as "King Philip," Native Americans took up arms against the colonists. King Philip's War raged across New England from New Hampshire to Connecticut in 1675 and 1676. By the time the fighting was done, thousands were dead, colonial villages lay in ruins, and Native American populations were devastated. In proportion to the population of the time, King Philip's War was the deadliest conflict ever fought on American soil.

One of the saddest chapters in this brutal tale occurred on the shores of Deer Island. It was to this island that the Massachusetts Bay Colony forcibly interned hundreds of Native Americans, known as "Praying Indians." Though they had converted to Christianity and pledged their loyalty to the English, the settlers feared the Praying Indians, many of them from the Nipmuc Tribe, would join in arms with the enemy. That fear quickly evolved into paranoia and bigotry, and during the middle of the night on October 30, 1675, the English hurried them from Natick and other "praying towns" around Boston onto boats along the Charles River in Watertown, ferrying them to Deer Island.

Some historical accounts place the number of prisoners at five hundred, but Native American oral traditions put the total much higher. Whatever the number, the Native Americans suffered great hardships during the particularly harsh winters of

PHILLIP alias METACOMET of Pokanoket
Engraved from the original as Published by Church

1675 and 1676. They were given few provisions, and subsisted on clams and other shellfish. They lacked adequate shelter from the bitter cold, but were not allowed to cut firewood. Colonial settlers were authorized to kill any Native American found off Deer Island not accompanied by an English guard. John Eliot (the minister who had converted the Native Americans) and Daniel Gookin visited in December 1675 and reported, "the island was bleak and cold, their wigwams poor and mean, their clothes few and thin."

Before they were released in May 1676, it is estimated that as many as half of the prisoners died from starvation or exposure. Many who survived were sold into slavery in the West Indies. Without question, it was one of the darkest moments in Boston's history, and one that continues to cast shadows on Deer Island. A Native American Memorial, scheduled to be unveiled on the island's southwest corner in 2011, depicts the suffering of three granite figures—a tribal elder along with a woman and child—huddled together under a blanket.

Little improved on Deer Island. In the late 1840s, Irish refugees fleeing the Great Famine sold all they had for a one-way ticket to America and an opportunity to finally be free of the disease and death that savaged their country. In 1847 alone, nearly 25,000 Irish citizens immigrated to Boston. By 1850, a third of the city's population was Irish.

So many refugees perished during the voyage that the vessels became known as "coffin ships." But the situation was equally desperate for those who survived the journey, arriving in Boston without money, their health, or a place to live. Many refugees took up residence in the poor, unsanitary neighborhoods near the waterfront, such as the North End. The utterly destitute camped outdoors on Boston Common. Boston was overwhelmed, and the sudden influx of the Irish was seen by many in Puritan Boston

VIEW OF THE NEW ALMS HOUSE for the CITY OF BOSTON in the STATE OF MASSACHUSETTS, ERECTING on DEER ISLAND in BOSTON HARBOR. 1849.
JOHN P. QUILCOX, ARCHITECT

The almshouse, circa 1849. Courtesy the Library of Congress.

as a threat to the city's economy, health, and way of life.

By the summer of 1847—the infamous Black '47—the quarantine station at Rainsford Island was no longer equipped to care for their sheer numbers. The city took possession of Deer Island for "sanitary purposes" and designated it as the new quarantine station. A hospital and associated buildings were built on the island's southern tip. Sick immigrants arriving in Boston were quarantined, though those who passed the initial inspection faced the prospect of being sent back to Deer Island if they became ill. Nearly five thousand refugees were quarantined between 1847 and 1850, and approximately eight hundred died on the island, an ocean away from the home they were forced to flee and on the doorstep of the city that held the promise of a new life.

As Boston continued to grow during the second half of the nineteenth century, residential areas began to spring up around some of the city's less palatable social institutions, such as its homes for the poor and juvenile offenders. As a result, the city relocated these "undesirable elements" to Deer Island. In addition to the quarantine station, which was moved to Gallops Island in 1860, Deer Island became home to the city's almshouse, house of industry, schools for paupers, and houses of reformation. By the 1880s, the island was a veritable Atlantic Alcatraz, this time for city criminals. And in 1904, the Hill Prison, one of the first institutions in the U.S. built specifically for women, opened its doors. That building later became the Suffolk County House of Correction and remained on the island until 1991.

Like so many other islands in the harbor, Deer Island provided military protection for Boston. The island played a minor role in the American Revolution, when, in June 1775, a small band of patriots raided the island and seized eight hundred sheep and lambs, a few heads of cattle, and a handful of British prisoners. In May 1776, a naval battle took place in Shirley Gut between the American privateer *Franklin*, commanded by Captain James Mugford, and the British fleet — still lingering in the harbor.

At the onset of World War II, Fort Dawes was built on the southern tip of Deer Island to monitor the harbor entrance. The fort was named in honor of Revolutionary

War hero William Dawes, who rode alongside Paul Revere. The Navy used the fort to operate a radar and signal station, and naval guns on the island were capable of reaching targets as far north as Gloucester and as far south as Plymouth. Later in the war, Fort Dawes controlled the electronically operated minefields in the north channel of Boston Harbor, and nets were stretched from Deer Island to Hull to prevent submarines and German U-boats from entering Boston Harbor.

With the exception of the 1880s steam-driven pumping station that was restored as a visitor center, all of the island's military and institutional structures are long gone, as the island's landscape was drastically altered to make way for the current plant. (To shield Winthrop residents from construction, the island's drumlin was even moved to its northern side.)

The new wastewater treatment plant occupies two-thirds of the island, but Deer Island offers more than sixty acres of parkland with five miles of public trails. A paved 2.6-mile walkway along the water, which is handicap accessible, provides views of the ocean, the islands, and the city five miles away. Fishing is permitted along the shoreline and in designated areas. Deer Island is a popular spot with local residents, so the small parking lot is often filled on pleasant days in all seasons.

The north side of the island offers a fantastic overlook of the Boston skyline, and from the top of the 135-foot hill, children of all ages will delight in following the planes coming in for landing at Logan International Airport. To the east of the overlook, near the water tower, is a simple granite bench on which "Rest Haven" is engraved. The bench honors the estimated 4,252 people buried on the island between 1847 and 1908—from the Irish immigrants who died at the quarantine station to the paupers and criminals unclaimed by relatives or friends. The cemetery was moved to this side of the island after the Army bought the island.

Despite brighter days, death seems to linger on Deer Island. During construction of the haul road for the wastewater treatment plant in the early 1990s, several unmarked graves were uncovered. The remains were taken to a funeral home in Rhode Island where they were kept until a summer day in 2001, when they were returned in

The Deer Island Pumping Station, built in 1895 and expanded in 1909, has since been restored as a visitor center. Courtesy the Library of Congress.

a hearse to Deer Island to be reinterred in a single casket. Construction work came to a halt as men were recruited as impromptu pallbearers. As the construction workers stood at attention, hard hats placed over their hearts, everyone lowered their heads in silent prayer.

From the southern tip of Deer Island tankers and cargo ships from around the world pass Deer Island Light, a slender brown beacon, five hundred yards offshore. The present light replaced a cast-iron lighthouse built in 1890 and dismantled in 1982. Mounted on the cylindrical base of the old lighthouse, the beacon marks the dangerous shoals at the northern edge of President Roads, the harbor's main shipping channel, which is abuzz with activity.

Set against the backdrop of the revitalized harbor, a memorial dedicated in October 2007 honors the late Federal District Court Judge A. David Mazzone. It was the judge's landmark ruling that led to the cleanup of Boston Harbor. No doubt Mazzone would be proud of how the new treatment plant has transformed Boston for the better, and how his push toward progress provided Deer Island with a shining moment of redemption in a history that was tortured for far too long.

Bruce Jacobson has been the Superintendent of the Boston Harbor Islands national park area since 2005. Few people have the same perspective as he does when it comes to the role of the National Park Service and what makes this park area so distinctive.

"What makes this park unique? Location, location, location. It's all about having this whole system of islands that was so influenced by an urban region. They are relatively natural environments or historic sites that are available to the public, and they are not only available, but you can get on the subway and you're there! So that's what makes it special, not to mention that we do have three National Historical Landmarks and wild areas.

"One of the things I remember from my undergraduate days is that the word 'recreation' breaks down into 're-creation.'

The opportunity for people to leave their environment and go out and sit or play in the outdoors is an important part of who we are as Americans. Reconnecting and re-creating ourselves and our relationships with the world happens in a lot of places. It can happen in churches and coffee shops, but the outdoors for me is key. And you compound that with the opportunity to do that on an island, and that's something different still. There's something about an island that gives you a whole different perspective on life. So I think the importance of the National Park Service is protecting these great spaces where people can come together as a community. The National Park Service protects spaces with national significance—the great outdoor areas that speak to the foundation of America."

Public tours of the Deer Island Wastewater Treatment Plant, operated by the Massachusetts Water Resources Authority (MWRA), are given the first Tuesday of each month between April and November. Tours begin at 9:30 AM. Call ahead of time: 617-660-7607. There is no admittance to the fenced-off treatment facility without prior approval. Visit: www.mwra.state.ma.us

 Members of the Nipmuc and other local tribes gather on Deer Island each October to commemorate the internment of their ancestors during King Philip's War. For more information, visit www.nipmucnation.org.

Dogs permitted on leash.

Directions: Deer Island is accessed by Tafts Avenue in Winthrop.

Latitude: 42° 21' 56.22" North
Longitude: 70° 58' 45.44" West

Snake Island

Snake Island, near Deer Island and just a few hundred yards from Winthrop, earned its name from its serpentine shape. Today, the island is owned by the town of Winthrop, and Snake Island has one of the largest remaining salt marshes in the Boston Harbor Islands. The mudflats and grassy clearings offer excellent offshore birding opportunities. In the late 1800s and early 1900s, lobstermen, clammers, and their families lived on the island seasonally. Today, licensed clammers harvest the productive mudflats between January and May. Access to Snake Island is easiest at high tide.

World's End

Bounded by the Weir River on the east and Hingham Harbor and its islands on the west, World's End occupies the tip of Cushing's Neck in the tony Boston suburb of Hingham. The drive down Martin's Lane to the reservation gives visitors just a taste of the lush scenery they will find inside the park, where a looping network of shady carriage paths evokes the grandeur of a seaside manor. This 248-acre reservation, one of the Boston Harbor "mainland" Islands, is graced with varied terrains of sandy coves, woodlands, fresh and saltwater marshes, grassy meadows, and granite cliffs. Such a bucolic setting makes World's End the perfect place to spend an afternoon, following the road wherever it may lead.

Until early European settlers built a causeway to connect it to the mainland, World's End proper—which occupies just a portion of the total reservation—became an island at high tide. From overhead, the shape of the reservation, with the sandy causeway connecting the double drumlins of World's End to two mainland drumlins, is very similar to Spectacle Island.

As on Spectacle Island, it is thought that Native Americans used World's End as a seasonal campsite. Native Americans set fish weirs and dug for shellfish on the island's shores. After European settlers arrived, the land was put to use by Hingham farmers for over three hundred years. No large-scale development ever occurred at World's End, though it certainly could have.

In 1855, John R. Brewer, a prominent Hingham resident, began acquiring parcels of land on Cushing's Neck, which he used to raise livestock and farm. By the 1880s, Brewer had acquired nearly all of the land that encompasses the present-day reservation, and his sprawling 400-acre farm included the family's mansion along Martin's Lane, stables, homes for the farmhands, a sheepfold, a smokehouse, and even a house for the family's guinea pigs, which were exhibited at local fairs. It seems Brewer always had an interest in landscape design, planting ornamental trees on Cushing's Neck soon after he bought the property, and in 1886 this pastime led him to hire America's most famous landscape architect, Frederick Law Olmsted.

Olmsted had already achieved considerable fame for his work on New York's Central Park when he moved to Brookline, Massachusetts in 1883. One cause for Olmsted's decision to relocate from New York to Brookline may have been his work on the twenty-year project we now know as Boston's Emerald Necklace, though it has been suggested as well that Olmsted was fond of Brookline because it embodied everything he believed a suburb should be. Though it might surprise some, given his success in having designed the nation's most celebrated public spaces, Olmsted was an early advocate of planned suburban communities that could combine the conveniences of cities with the charms of rural life. "No great town can long exist without great suburbs," he wrote in 1868.

Under Brewer's commission, Olmsted was hired to subdivide World's End into residential parcels. Although Brewer had no immediate intention of selling these parcels off, he wanted to be prepared in case he ran into financial difficulty. Olmsted's design for 163 subplots of varying sizes was Brewer's contingency plan.

Like many of the Boston Harbor Islands, World's End in the 1880s was relatively barren from centuries of agricultural use. It was Olmsted's pet interest in reforesting the islands that attracted him to Brewer's project. Olmsted desired to keep the pasture and meadow land open, so he didn't intend to plant groves of native trees that would eventually become a dense forest. Instead, his layout called for a network of curvilinear roads that hugged the natural contours of the drumlins and were lined by tall, stately trees such as English oaks, Norway maples, and American elms.

The Brewers built the cart paths and planted the tree seedlings fairly closely to Olmsted's original specifications. (The tree planting also extended to Sarah and Langlee Islands in Hingham Harbor, owned by the Brewer family at the time.) However, no subplot was ever sold, presumably because it wasn't a financial necessity. This partial execution of Olmsted's proposal has left the property with a system of roads that appear to lead nowhere, which can be charming and peculiar at the same time. After the Brewer family line died out in 1936, most of the property's buildings, including the mansion, were torn down and World's End fell into relative disuse.

It's hard to imagine, but this nearly realized subdivision was once under consideration as the potential home of the United Nations. In 1945, the newly created international organization settled on the United States as the location for its headquarters, and metropolitan Boston and New York City were the two leading contenders. The United Nations' site committee ruled out any urban locations because of its sizable land requirements, and Massachusetts Governor Maurice Tobin formed a committee to identify possible suburban locations for the world body. World's End was one of the sites on the initial list because of its availability of land and proximity to Boston, though it failed to make the final cut. (It certainly gives one pause to think of the United Nations headquartered in an area called World's End.)

However, other suburban Boston locations were still being considered when millionaire philanthropist John D. Rockefeller, Jr. swooped in at the last minute and shocked everyone with a gift of six blocks of Manhattan real estate along the East

River. Even though the committee from the start had eliminated all sites within ten miles of Manhattan, it reversed itself in a New York minute and accepted Rockefeller's gift, once again leaving Boston, its civic rival to the north, in the shadows of Gotham.

Twenty years after the United Nations flirtation, proposals were drawn to build a nuclear power plant on World's End, but it was eventually constructed in Plymouth. With the property under increasing threat of development, more than $450,000 was raised from public subscription to purchase it. In 1967, World's End was bought by the Trustees of Reservations—one of the oldest private land trusts in the world, conceived in 1891 by Olmsted's protégée and partner Charles Eliot.

Now that the seedlings have grown and saplings have matured, visitors to World's End can enjoy the fulfillment of the landscape that Olmsted designed more than a

Though it is most often associated with tree-lined paths, World's End also offers wide open meadows with plenty of big sky.

century ago. It's very easy for your eyes to remain focused on the rutted road ahead as it ascends and descends numerous hills and gracefully curves with the rolls of the land, but those who focus solely on the road ahead will miss out on spectacular water views, framed by the trees of which Olmsted was so fond.

The Rocky Neck section of World's End provides a much different feel from the broad, tree-lined carriage paths and open meadows found elsewhere in the reservation. With narrow trails that thread their way under a dense canopy of trees and along granite outcrops, Rocky Neck is much wilder and feels a little like the Maine coastline. What begins as a walk through the deep woods, where you wander through cobwebs and brush up against scrubby pine, ends with the meeting of land and water. Emerging onto the rocky precipices along the Weir River, you are confronted by the condominiums and homes along Nantasket Beach. Had Olmsted and Brewer's subdivision come to pass, it may have fit right in with these other residential developments. During the summer, the river is a popular anchoring spot for weekend boaters, and the chatter of sailors and the hum of jet-skis fills the air.

World's End is filled with recreational opportunities throughout the year, and the Trustees of Reservations offers a wide variety of educational programming for nature lovers and families. It is a birder's paradise, providing habitats for grassland-

In 1886, Frederick Law Olmsted described the Boston Harbor Islands, after centuries of deforestation, as "Artificially bald, raw, bleak, prosaic, inhospitable." When the Pilgrims explored Boston Harbor in 1621, they found that Native Americans had cleared some of the islands from end to end to support their seasonal camps. After the Europeans settled in Boston, they further denuded the islands for their wood and transformed their landscapes to support farming and grazing.

Olmsted sought to restore the islands to their original vegetative state and argued that the attractiveness of Boston Harbor and its islands "reckoned no insignificant element of the trade and prosperity of the city." In addition, he reasoned that the lack of trees made the islands more susceptible to extreme weather conditions and contributed to their erosion into the sea.

"Once the islands were bodies of foliage," Olmsted wrote in an 1886 article in *The Century*. "Seen one against another and grouping with wood headlands, they formed scenery of grace and amenity, cheerful, genial, hospitable. But long ago they were despoiled for petty private gains. It would not lessen but enhance their values for these purposes to dress them again with the graces of naturally disposed foliage; and under a well-prepared system, patiently followed, it would cost little more every year to do this than is spent for an hour's exhibition of fireworks."

Olmsted submitted a formal report to the Boston Park Commissioners for the reforestation of the islands. Olmsted did not propose to turn the barren islands into landscaped "parks" similar to the Emerald Necklace, and no land was to be purchased. The plan was simply to plant native trees—such as pine, birch, and oak—on about four hundred acres at a cost of $5,000 a year for six years. The Park Commissioners, presumably more interested in investing civic money in pyrotechnic displays, rejected Olmsted's plan.

Although many of the harbor islands are again green with vegetation, the native habitats were never formally restored. Many of the islands' trees are invasive species or scrubby, pioneer species, such as staghorn sumac, that are among the first plants to return to an area that has been disturbed by activities such as agriculture and deforestation. Building on Olmsted's vision, park management is leading habitat restoration projects to eradicate invasive species and allow native vegetation to reclaim the islands.

nesting birds and is a great spot for viewing landbird migration, such as waterfowl, raptors, and herons. The restoration of tidal flow to a salt marsh dammed by settlers hundreds of years ago is helping to revive its ecosystem. Kayakers and fishermen can explore the miles of coastline along the reservation or venture to the islands in Hingham Harbor. The four miles of gravel carriageways and grassy trails are a natural draw for both walkers and joggers, while the benches scattered throughout the property and along the shore provide spots to rest and relax. In the winter, the snow-covered trails are popular with cross-country skiers.

The reservation is particularly exquisite in the fall when a vibrant palette emerges among Olmsted's trees. Walking through the wooded areas of Rocky Neck in autumn will bring to mind the opening stanza of Robert Frost's poem "The Road Not Taken":

Two roads diverged in a yellow wood, / And sorry I could not travel both / And be one traveler, long I stood / And looked down one as far I could / To where it bent in the undergrowth...

The good news is that, unlike the traveler in Frost's poem, you don't have to fret about which road to take at World's End. If you have the time, you can travel them all.

ADDITIONAL INFORMATION

 Dogs permitted on leash.

🅢 Mountain biking permitted on dirt roads.

Horseback riding permitted with purchase of an annual permit from The Trustees of Reservations. (Cost of permit is approximately $100.)

Summer solstice celebration in June, guided kayak expeditions, and ecology programs for children and families. See Events section of The Trustees of Reservations website or phone 781-740-6665 for additional events.
www.thetrustees.org

Admission: Free for children and members of The Trustees of Reservations. $5 for nonmember adults.

Directions: From Route 3, take exit 14 and follow Route 228 north toward Hingham for 6.5 miles. Turn left onto Route 3A and follow for 0.4 miles. Turn right onto Summer Street and, at the major intersection with Rockland Street, continue straight across onto Martin's Lane. Follow for 0.7 miles until it dead ends at the entrance.

Webb Memorial State Park

On a summer evening, the lot at Webb Memorial State Park is full, and walkers and joggers converge on the gravel paths snaking through the park. Fishermen unwind in chairs along the stony beach, waiting for the fish to bite, while picnickers spread their blankets alongside the carpet of yellow, white, and purple wildflowers filling the meadows. With such magnificent scenery, it's no wonder this recreation area is so popular with local North Weymouth residents.

Named in honor of a former Weymouth police captain, Webb Memorial State Park occupies a peninsula extending into Hingham Bay at the end of Weymouth Neck, flanked by the Fore River to the west and the Back River to the east. Until the area around George Lane Beach was filled in, the peninsula became an island at high tide when the Back River cut it off from the rest of Weymouth. Watching local residents and other visitors enjoying the tranquil park today, it's hard to imagine that as recently as the 1960s this piece of land was home to something much different—a noisy, smelly fertilizer plant.

Weymouth Neck was used as a seasonal campsite by Native Americans, and it was part of an area they called "Wessagussett," Algonquian for "by the small saltwater cove." Europeans principally used the land for agriculture until 1861, when the Bradley Fertilizer Company moved in and built a massive complex of buildings along the bank of the Back River. In addition to the factory, facilities included a blacksmith shop, furnaces, wharves, and grease extraction tanks. Indeed, the Bradley Fertilizer Company was quite an operation, capitalizing on the quintessentially American quest to maintain a green expanse of lawn—which isn't as modern a phenomenon as you

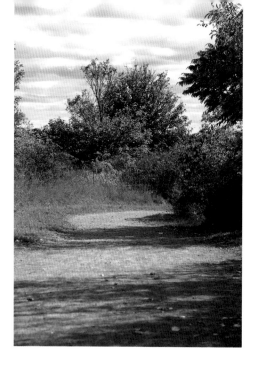

might think. Bradley's advertisements, even back in the 1890s, admonished consumers that "a rusty, uneven faded out lawn is a disgrace to any true American."

It is somewhat ironic that something as lovely and refreshing as a green, grassy yard could be the end result of such a squalid production process. While the company boasted that its fertilizers combined the "quick action of Peruvian guano and the lasting properties of bone," it was the smell of the raw materials used in the production process—including bones, fish scraps, animal hides, and dried blood—that earned the area around the plant the nickname of "Skunk Island." Worse than the smell, perhaps, were the hazardous consequences that came from the plant's large-scale mixing of chemicals, such as a fire in 1946 that melted the factory's acid tanks. The acid was so strong that the roads caught flame and two fire trucks responding to the scene had to be abandoned because the acid ate through their tires. Despite this, the fertilizer factory did not close until 1966.

Just as other Boston Harbor Islands have been used for military fortifications since the Puritans dropped anchor, Weymouth Neck played a role in protecting Boston from potential attacks as well—though this time it was during the Cold War. In 1954, the federal government purchased a site on the peninsula and built a Nike missile base.

During the Cold War era, threat of foreign attack on American soil shifted from the sea to the air. The nation's coastal defenses came to rely heavily on the Nike anti-aircraft missile system, which was not only the most expensive missile system ever deployed, but also the most widespread, with three hundred sites in thirty states. Sites were chosen to protect urban areas throughout the United States, bringing a little bit of Doctor Strangelove to suburbs such as Weymouth. The missiles, capable of carrying small nuclear warheads, were stored in underground silos and controlled by a radar system on what is now Spinnaker Island, across Hingham Bay.

Right: From 1861 until the 1960s, the Bradley Fertilizer Company and other chemical manufacturers occupied a large portion of Weymouth Neck. Pictured here are illustrations from the company's almanac of 1883.

The missile site (located on the west side of Webb Memorial State Park) was deactivated in the 1970s, and the property was transferred to the Commonwealth of Massachusetts. The property was landscaped and converted to parkland, and Webb Memorial State Park officially opened in 1980.

However, the park was still plagued by a dreadful legacy of environmental contamination left behind by both the Bradley Fertilizer Company and the American Agricultural Chemical Co., which bought the site in 1900. Long before the idea of the park came to be, both companies buried industrial waste, such as iron oxide, lead sulfate sludge, coal ash, and animal bones.

ConocoPhillips, which acquired American Agricultural Chemical Co., spearheaded an extensive environmental cleanup of the park that took place between 2005 and 2008. Just as Spectacle Island has been transformed from its checkered past as a dumping ground to parkland, so too has Webb Memorial State Park been reborn as a recreational area for all to enjoy. Landscaping and restoration work has made the park even more popular as a walking and picnicking site. The contaminated soil has been capped, and there are new trees, shrubs, overlooks, and benches throughout. Walking trails and restrooms have been upgraded, and wetlands have been restored.

As with most of the Boston Harbor Islands, Webb Memorial State Park consists of drumlins formed by glaciers, although much of the original topography has been altered by grading and landscaping. Despite its small size, the park contains a wide variety of landscapes, such as meadows of wildflowers, groves of sumac and birch trees, and wetlands filled with cattails. Although swimming is not permitted, the

One of the more moving monuments at Webb Memorial State Park honors Commander Donald F. Haviland of the United States Merchant Marine. When World War II broke out, Haviland was nearing the age of fifty and too old to re-enlist in the Marines. Undeterred, he volunteered for the Merchant Marine instead. The Merchant Marine's delivery of supplies provided a critical lifeline to the Allies during the war, and missions were so perilous that they suffered a higher proportion of casualties than any other service, except the Marines.

Born in Weymouth, Haviland served as chief engineer on the SS *Henry Bacon*, which transported war supplies and Norwegian war refugees between the Soviet Union and Britain in February 1945. A heavy gale in the Arctic Ocean forced the *Henry Bacon* to drop out of its 44-ship convoy. Alone and vulnerable off the Norwegian coast, it came under attack by German bombers and began to sink. The Norwegians and some crew, including Haviland, filled the lifeboats, but they simply couldn't accommodate the remaining personnel.

When this situation became known to Haviland, he insisted on giving his place to an eighteen-year-old messman from Revere, pleading with him, "Come on, kid, get into that damn lifeboat!" Shortly thereafter, he and fourteen other crew members went down with the ship. Haviland posthumously received the Merchant Marine's highest honor. He was also honored by the Soviet Union and Norway.

A plaque in the park tells Haviland's story, and the adjacent flagpole, which can be seen in the harbor areas around Weymouth Neck, proudly flies the colors of the United States and the Merchant Marine. The water of the Back River is an appropriate backdrop for honoring this mariner and hero.

beaches are good spots from which to launch your kayak to explore the islands in Hingham Bay.

A granite block across the channel from Grape Island commemorates the Grape Island Alarm of May 1775 and salutes the Weymouth militiamen who "repulsed an attempt by the British to secure supplies from Grape Island for General Howe's beleaguered army in Boston." However, it's the smaller memorials to prominent Weymouth citizens and civic leaders spread throughout this well-loved recreation area that demonstrate its connection to the local residents. And as a visit to Webb Memorial State Park on a summer evening will attest, that connection is even stronger now that the park has been revitalized.

ADDITIONAL INFORMATION

 Dogs permitted on leash.

Directions:
Take Route 3A to Weymouth, turn north on Neck Street, and follow to the end.

Nut Island

"We ain't baking cookies here!" That's the caustic response local residents received when they complained about the powerful stench emanating from Nut Island's old wastewater treatment plant. For nearly a century, Nut Island was home to facilities that spewed under-treated wastewater into Quincy Bay, and it certainly wasn't anyone's idea of a recreation area.

How times have changed! Thanks to the replacement of the wastewater treatment plant, a key component in the overall cleanup of Boston Harbor, Nut Island has been revitalized and is now a delightful place to visit. Anglers cast their lines off the long fishing pier. Paved paths along the shoreline provide walkers and joggers with pleasant views. And any smell in the air now is likely to be the fragrance of colorful wildflowers or the salty breeze coming off the harbor.

Nut Island, once separated from the mainland by a sandbar that disappeared at high tide, is now a peninsula firmly attached to the end of Houghs Neck, a tight-knit Quincy neighborhood whose bluffs provide fantastic views of the harbor and Boston skyline. In the late 1800s and early 1900s, Houghs Neck was a popular summer resort with lively social affairs drawing Bostonians and tourists from all around New England, and these vacationers often spent the day swimming and picnicking on nearby Nut Island.

In the latter half of the nineteenth century this cavorting gave way to a spookier pastime. Nearly a half century after Donald McKay and others had given rise to a proud shipbuilding history across the harbor, Nut Island was turned into a graveyard for a vast number of sailing vessels, including steamers and some of the Navy's most powerful and historic ships from the Civil War. Thomas Butler & Co., a marine junk company, purchased the ships, towed them to Nut Island, and grounded them on the beach. Workers stripped them of their engines and other components, removed every piece of iron, brass, and copper, and sent the valuable material back to Boston for resale. Then, all that remained of these once-proud ships was set ablaze to salvage any remaining metal, with the devouring flames oftentimes illuminating the night sky, providing a spectacular sight for crowds that lined the hills and shores for miles around.

The first of the ships to meet their ignominious end at Nut Island was the steam frigate USS *Niagara* in the 1880s. The *Niagara*, the largest wooden ship in the world when it was launched in the 1850s, served in the Civil War and was one of the two vessels that laid the first trans-Atlantic telegraph cable. Other warships that returned to the sea at Nut Island included the USS *Wyoming*, the USS *Brooklyn*, and the USS *Galena*, one of the first Civil War ironclads and a sister ship of the famous USS *Monitor*.

The *Brooklyn* gained its fame as part of the fleet under the command of Civil War hero David Farragut, whose statue stands watch over Pleasure Bay in South Boston. The *Brooklyn* saw action in heated Civil War battles, including the capture of both New Orleans and Mobile. During the Battle of Mobile Bay the *Brooklyn* watched as the USS *Tecumseh* struck a tethered naval mine (known at the time as a "torpedo"). Seeing this unfolding calamity, the *Brooklyn* wavered as it was about to enter the bay.

It was this hesitation that supposedly caused Farragut (who was reportedly lashed to the rigging of the USS *Hartford*) to give the order, "Damn the torpedoes! Full speed ahead!"

Some of the cottages on Houghs Neck were built with relics of these doomed warships and steamers. Pilot houses, cabin doors, windows, and other salvaged parts were incorporated into the cottages on Houghs Neck, making for a quirky architectural hodgepodge.

The Houghs Neck residents endured some noisy days during the 1870s when Nut Island was used to test some of the largest cannons ever seen at that time. These massive fifteen-inch guns were cast at the South Boston Iron Company foundry, which had been supplying ordnance to the military since the War of 1812. The gunnery experiments were conducted by Colonel Norman Wiard, a well-known inventor of guns and projectiles who was frequently consulted by President Lincoln during the Civil War.

Wiard's monster cannons used the eroding bluffs of Princes Head on Peddocks Island for target practice. Hundreds of people, including American military officers and artillery experts, watched in awe as the booming cannons, weighing more than twenty tons, thundered with every test. The guns hurtled 500-pound shots, which—when successful—pierced the solid wrought-iron target plates on Princes Head about a mile across the water. However, these experiments didn't always go as planned. On one occasion, the ordnance sailed over the target and landed in a cemetery in Hull. The experiments cost nearly half a million dollars, and Wiard would later come under criticism for giving false reports of success and fleecing the government out of $250,000 by engaging in extravagant expenditures during his summers in Boston.

Today, these experiments are commemorated with a modest monument set against the backdrop of Princes Head. The centerpiece of the monument is a small, rusted remnant of an 11-inch Rodman rifled cannon that burst during a test-firing. It is flanked by two projectiles used in that type of cannon.

Around the turn of the twentieth century, Nut Island became home to a sewage pump station. It was replaced in 1952 by a wastewater treatment facility, but the plant's open concrete tanks and discharge into the bay long assaulted the eyes and noses of the "Neckers," residents of the Houghs Neck neighborhood.

Ironically, bottom-feeding fish such as flounder—with apologies to The Standells, who coined the infamous lyrics—"loved that dirty water." They flourished in the warm water and sludge discharged by the old treatment plants and, somewhat dubiously, Houghs Neck became known as the "Flounder Capital of the World," attracting fishermen from as far away as South Carolina. Eventually, though, the fish—like the Neckers—had enough of the pollution.

As part of the massive Boston Harbor cleanup, the offensive wastewater treatment plant on Nut Island was replaced by a new headworks facility in 1998. This headworks removes large objects as well as sand and gravel from sewage piped from twenty-one communities south and west of Boston. The screened wastewater is then pumped through a 4.8-mile tunnel under Boston Harbor to Deer Island for treatment.

Thanks in large part to the sustained activism of the Neckers, along with the opening of the headworks facility, Nut Island became a revitalized, landscaped park area in 1999. Silver vents dotting the park are reminders that sewage treatment operations continue at Nut Island, but the red-brick headworks building, with its sloping green

The $4.5-billion cleanup of Boston Harbor has been the catalyst for the revitalization of the Boston Harbor Islands. The new facilities, built and operated by the Massachusetts Water Resources Authority (MWRA), have reversed the deteriorating water quality and made Boston Harbor one of the cleanest in the United States. MWRA's wastewater facilities serve forty-three communities, nearly half of the population of Massachusetts, and the amount of sewage treated by the MWRA system is enough to fill the Prudential Building three times each day.

But how exactly does the wastewater treatment process work? First, sewage is transported to headworks facilities, such as the one on Nut Island, where grit and large objects are removed. Pumps then send the wastewater to the treatment plant on Deer Island.

At Deer Island, preliminary treatment allows for the settling of mud and sand, which is taken to a landfill for environmentally safe disposal. Then, the wastewater flows to primary settling tanks where up to 60 percent of the solids settle as a mixture of sludge and water. After that, secondary treatment occurs; oxygen is added to speed the growth of microbes that will consume the waste before it settles to the bottom of secondary tanks. The remaining sludge is then processed in those gigantic, landmark egg digesters, which mimic our own digestion process (in fact, the temperature is maintained at ninety-eight degrees) to break the sludge down into methane gas, carbon dioxide, solid organic byproducts, and water. The two geodesic dome tanks at Deer Island store the methane, which is used to help power the plant.

The remaining sludge—which is 94 percent water—is pumped back under the harbor to the Fore River pelletizing facility in Quincy through a 14-inch pipe. There it is dewatered, heat-dried, and converted into fertilizer pellets, which can be applied to crops, lawns, and gardens. The remaining wastewater is disinfected, and the effluent is discharged east of Deer Island into Massachusetts Bay by means of a 9.5-mile outfall tunnel more than 250 feet below the ocean floor. Toward the end of the tunnel, more than fifty release points allow the dilution of the effluent in deeper waters off the coast.

roof, descends four stories underground and is eclipsed by the beauty of the surroundings.

Although it's small and parking is limited, Nut Island offers plenty of opportunities to enjoy the harbor.

Trails lead to views of other harbor islands, as well as Quincy Bay to the west and Hingham Bay to the east. Evening is a particularly pleasant time to visit. As the sun sets near the Boston skyline, fishermen cast their lines in hopes of nabbing some of the rebounding populations of flounder, striped bass, and bluefish.

During the summer, a golden blanket of wildflowers runs to the edge of the (now) blue sea. There are over twenty species of wildflowers at Nut Island, including Queen Anne's lace, lupine, coreopsis, dianthus, Indian paint brush, and gaillardia. Wild roses, day lilies, and buttercups also provide pockets of color throughout the park. In a sign of how much things have changed in recent years, Nut Island now hosts an annual wildflower festival. It's true that you still may not smell cookies at Nut Island, but you can certainly stop and smell the flowers.

ADDITIONAL INFORMATION

Dogs permitted on leash.

Directions: From Boston, take I-93 south to Route 3A south (Exit 12). Stay on Route 3A south for approximately three miles and take a left on Sea Street. Stay on Sea Street to the end and turn left on Sea Avenue to the entrance to the park.

Harbor

& Island Resources

Get Involved!

Boston Harbor Island Alliance

In November 1996, Congress made the Boston Harbor Islands a unit of the National Park System with a new management philosophy: a public/private model for park development and funding. The Boston Harbor Island Alliance is one of the many organizations in the Boston Harbor Islands Partnership—which includes federal, state, city, and nonprofit agencies. Boston Harbor Island Alliance's primary objective is to ensure that people enjoy and use the resources of the park. "Our vision for the islands is that they will be integral to the life of the city," says Tom Powers, President of the Boston Harbor Island Alliance, "and that people think of going to the islands for lunch or for a drink at sunset. Maybe there's an artists' colony on one and a performing arts center on another, and events like the Regatta draw people from all over."

Most of the programming on the Boston Harbor Islands is supported by Boston Harbor Island Alliance. The popular Sunday afternoon jazz concerts on Spectacle Island are their brainchild, as is the Boston Harbor Islands Regatta, held every September. In terms of capital projects, the Island Alliance spearheaded construction of the new visitor center on Georges Island and a new $5.5 million pavilion on the Rose Kennedy Greenway that serves as a gateway to the islands. Visitors to the pavilion can purchase ferry tickets and view interactive exhibits, interpretive panels, and a granite topographical map of the islands inlaid in the ground.

"We are always looking for ideas with the theme of attracting visitors, but particularly kids, to the islands," says Powers.

Working with the National Park Service, and Massachusetts Department of Conservation and Recreation, Boston Harbor Island Alliance sponsors summer Family Fun Days. Activities are diverse: from art lessons and kite making, to fishing lessons and introductions to green technology. However, much goes on behind the scenes, too. The organization coordinates fundraising efforts, lobbies on behalf of the park, and supports the youth after-school program, Island Ambassadors, and educational programming.

In 1998, Captain David Weinstein founded Harbor Connections, a curriculum-based education program that turns the islands into living classrooms for students in Boston Public Schools and nearby towns. Now the Education Director for the Boston Harbor Island Alliance, Weinstein's programs bring more than 3,300 students a year out to the harbor islands for interdisciplinary learning. "Individually, each island provides a discrete laboratory where students can discover the rich diversity of life. But the lessons we teach extend beyond the classroom. We also encourage citizenship and stewardship in the students by introducing them to a public resource. We want them to feel the responsibility for taking care of the islands and make it a part of their neighborhood."

To access curriculums, educators should visit www.nps.gov/boha and link to "For Teachers." For more information on the Island Alliance: www.islandalliance.org.

Friends of the Boston Harbor Islands

The Friends of the Boston Harbor Islands are common sights on any island excursion, giving tours and staffing information booths. The Friends also assist park managers by clearing trails, undertaking improvement projects, and advocating for the islands' preservation. In addition, the Friends of the Boston Harbor Islands organize boat trips to islands not frequented by ferry service, such as Rainsford and Great Brewster Islands, and their New Year's Day island cruise is now a Boston Harbor tradition.

The Friends evolved from the efforts of the Boston Harbor Islands Volunteer Corps, organized in 1979 by Suzanne Gall Marsh. Nearly twenty years before the creation of the national park area, the Friends were the early champions of the harbor islands. Today, there are nearly five hundred members. Some members commit hundreds of hours each year, simply out of their love of the islands, and there are Friends who've been with the organization since its inception. "It's fascinating to realize the longevity of the volunteers who are involved," says Suzanne Gall Marsh. "There are people who have been involved for more than twenty-five years, and have gotten their children and grandchildren involved. Volunteers focus on whatever they're interested in. Some people hack down sumac, others greet visitors on the dock, and others work behind the scenes."

"The Friends have been a very positive force in people's lives, and people have become personal friends. I'm just so proud to be part of a group of people who love this place and have done such good things for it."

To get involved with the Friends: www.fbhi.org.

Volunteering

The National Park Service coordinates the volunteer services of many partners, such as United States Coast Guard Auxiliary, Friends of the Boston Harbor Islands, and corporate and community groups. The park offers many volunteer opportunities including a variety of citizen science projects, which provide hands-on opportunities for members of the community to connect with nature while contributing to scientific research.

For more information, visit: www.harborislands.org. Call: 617-223-8666 or email: BOHA_Information@nps.gov.

Resources

Boston Harbor Transportation

Boston Harbor Islands Ferry
Long Wharf
Boston, MA 02110
617-223-8666
www.harborislands.org

Boston Harbor Water Taxi
Boston, MA
617-593-9168
www.massport.com
🐾 *Operates between Logan Airport dock
and landings in Boston Harbor*

City Water Taxi
Boston, MA 02196
617-887-0321
www.citywatertaxi.com

Rowes Wharf Water Transport
60 Rowes Wharf
Boston, MA 02110
617-406-8584 (reservations, captain)
617-261-6620 (office, charters, groups)
www.roweswharfwatertransport.com

Boston's Best Cruises
116 East Howard Street
Quincy, MA 02169
617-770-0040
www.bostonsbestcruises.com

Cruises / Dining & Entertainment

Boston Belle Charters, Inc.
333 Victory Road
Quincy, MA 02171
617-592-6866
www.bostonbellecharters.com

Boston Harbor Cruises
One Long Wharf
Boston, MA 02110
617-227-4321
877-733-9425 (toll free)
www.bostonharborcruises.com
🐾 *Whale Watch*

Boston Island Charters
Captain John Dinga
617-645-0971
www.bostonislandscharters.com
captainjohn@comcast.net
🐾 *Departing from Quincy, Downtown
Boston, Georges Island and other locations.
Specializes in the outer islands — including
lobster bakes on the deserted island of
your choice!*

Boston Seaport Boat Charters
290 Northern Avenue
Boston, MA 02210
617-261-6633
www.bostonseaportboatcharters.com
🐾 *Whale Watch*

Liberty Boston
67 Long Wharf
Boston, MA 02110
617-742-0333
www.libertyfleet.com

Mass Bay Lines
60 Rowes Wharf
Boston, MA 02110
617-542-8000
www.massbaylines.com
🐾 *Whale Watch*

Odyssey Cruises
60 Rowes Wharf
Boston, MA 02110
866-307-2469
www.odysseycruises.com

Rowes Wharf Water Transport
60 Rowes Wharf
Boston, MA 02110
617-406-8584 (reservations, captain)
617-261-6620 (office, charters, groups)
www.roweswharfwatertransport.com

Spirit of Boston
Commonwealth Pier
200 Seaport Boulevard
Boston, MA 02210
866-211-3807 (individuals)
617-748-1400 (group)
www.spiritcruises.com

Water Transportation Alternatives Inc.
703 Washington Street
Quincy, MA 02169
617-222-6999
www.harborexpress.com

Recreation

Diving

Boston Harbor Diving Services
256 Marginal Street
East Boston, MA 02128
617-846-5151
www.bostondiving.com
🐾 *Certification & Diving Excursions*

Coastal Dive Center
191 Beal Street
Hingham, MA 02043
617-529-4317
www.coastaldivecenter.com
🐾 *Certification & Diving Excursions*

Mass Diving
247 West Central Street
Natick, MA 01760
508-651-0698
www.massdiving.com
🐾 *Certification*

Fishing Charters

B-Fast Fishing Charters
Rowes Wharf
Boston, MA 02110
781-293-6402
www.bfastcharters.com

Boston Fishstix
Marina Bay
Quincy, MA 02171
617-233-6090 Capt. Rich
978-314-2424 Capt. John
www.bostonfishstix.com

Boston Sportfishing
Mederios Dock
696 East 1st Street
South Boston, MA 02127
617-775-7745 (land line)
617-365-8610
www.bosotnsportfishing.com

Captain Fred Christian
505 Paradise Road
Swampscott, MA 01907
978-745-5339
www.captainfred.com

City Slicker Charters
Crystal Cove Marina
529 Shirley Street
Winthrop, MA 02152
781-641-3474
www.bostonboat.com

C.J. Victoria
Winthrop Town Pier
707 Shirley Street
Winthrop, MA 02152
617-283-5801
www.cjvictoria.com

Firefly Outfitters
One Federal Street
Boston, MA 02110
617-423-3474
www.fireflyoutfitters.com

Flying Fish Charters
238 Winthrop Shore Drive
Winthrop, MA 02152
617-909-0912
www.flyingfishchartersinc.com

Good Times Charters
Constitution Marina on Boston Harbor
Boston, MA 02110
617-435-4126
www.bostoncharters.com

Midnight Charter
83 Merryknoll Road
Weymouth, MA 02191
617-653-3772
www.charterfishboston.com

Reel Dream Charters
Marina Bay
333 Victory Road
Quincy, MA 02171
617-909-7122
www.reeldreamcharters.com

Roccus Charters
119 Danehill Road
Newton, MA 02461
617-956-4833 (Land Line)
781-316-4050 (Cell)
www.roccuscharters.com

*Kayaking, Canoeing, Sail Boats & Row Boat
Rentals/Lessons*

Billington Sea Kayak
41 Branch Point Road
Plymouth, MA 02360
508-746-5644
www.billingtonseakayak.com
🌿 *Kayak & Canoe—rentals & lessons*

Black Rock Sailing School
Fan Pier Marina
56 E Service Rd
South Boston, MA 02210
617-639-3061
www.blackrocksailingschool.com
🌿 *Sailing Lessons*

Boston Harbor Sailing Club
Rowes Wharf
Boston, MA 02110
617-720-0049
www.bostonharborsailing.com
🌿 *Sailing—Rentals & Lessons*

Boston Sailing Center
54 Lewis Wharf
Boston, MA 02110
617-227-4198
www.bostonsailingcenter.com
🌿 *Sailing—Rentals & Lessons*

Charles River Canoe & Kayak
2401 Commonwealth Avenue
Newton, MA 02466
617-965-5110
www.paddleboston.com
🌿 *Kayak & Canoe—Rentals, Lessons
& Guided Tours*

Community Boating, Inc.
21 David Mugar Way
Boston, MA 02114
617-523-1038
www.community-boating.org
🌿 *Sailing, Windsurfing & Kayaking
—rentals & lessons*

Courageous Sailing Center
Charlestown Navy Yard
Pier Four
Boston, MA 02129
617-268-7243
www.courageoussailing.org
🌿 *Sailing Lessons*

Hingham Bay Racing
Hingham, MA 02043
www.hbphrf.org

Hingham Shipyard Marinas
24 Shipyard Drive
Hingham, MA 02043
781-749-6647
www.hinghamshipyardmarinas.com
Kayak Rentals

Lincoln Maritime Center
1-5 Steamboat Lane
Hingham, MA 02043
781-741-5225
www.lincolnmaritime.org
Sailing and Rowing Lessons

Piers Park Sailing
95 Marginal Street
East Boston, MA 02128
617-561-6677
www.piersparksailing.org
Lessons & Adaptive Sailing Program

SailTime
Fan Pier
1 Marina Park Drive
Boston, MA 02210
617-899-6815
www.sailtime.com
Sailing—Rentals and Charters

The Nahant Dory Club
Tudor Wharf
Nahant, MA 01908
www.doryclub.org
Sailing Lessons & Racing

U.S. Coast Guard Auxiliary
www.nws.cgaux.org
Boating Courses

United States Power Squadrons
www.usps.org
Boating Courses

Wild Turkey Paddlers
www.wtpaddlers.org
Informational Kayaking Group—Biweekly Skill Sessions

Marinas

Admirals Hill Marina
305 Commandants Way
Chelsea, MA 02150
617-889-4002
www.admiralshillmarina.com

Bay Pointe Marina
64 Washington Court
Quincy, MA 02169
617-471-1777
www.baypointe-marina.com

Boston Bay Marina
84 Condor Street
East Boston, MA 02128
617-569-5212
www.bostonbaymarina.com

Boston Harbor Shipyard & Marina
256 Marginal Street
East Boston, MA 02128
617-561-1400
www.bhsmarina.com

Boston Waterboat Marina
66 Long Wharf (North Side)
Boston, MA 02110
617-523-1027
www.bostonwaterboatmarina.com

Boston Yacht Haven
87 Commercial Wharf
Boston, MA 02110
617-367-5050
www.byhonline.com

Captain's Cove Marina
100 Cove Way
Quincy, MA 02269
617-328-3331
www.captainscovemarina.com

Cohasset Harbor Marina
33 Parker Avenue
Cohasset, MA 02025
781-337-1964
www.cohassetharbormarina.com

Constitution Marina
28 Constitution Road
Boston, MA 02129
617-241-9640
www.constitutionmarina.com

Hingham Shipyard Marinas
24 Shipyard Drive
Hingham, MA 02043
781-749-6647
www.hinghamshipyardmarinas.com

Pirates Cove Marina
3 Otis Street
Hingham, MA 02043
781-254-2821
www.piratescovemarineservices.com

Seaport Landing Marina
154 Lynnway
Lynn, MA 01901
781-592-5821
www.ci.lynn.ma.us

Shipyard Quarters Marina
1 Pier Eight
Charlestown, MA 02129
857-452-7221
www.shipyardquartersmarina.com

Spectacle Island Marina
28 Constitution Road
Boston, MA 02129
857-452-7221
www.constitutionmarina.com

Steamboat Wharf Marina
48 George Washington Blvd.
Hull, MA 02045
781-925-0044
www.steamboatwharfmarina.com

Tern Harbor Marina
275 River Street
Weymouth, MA 02191
781-337-1964
www.ternharbormarina.com

The Marina at Rowes Wharf
50 Rowes Wharf
Boston, MA 02110
617-748-5013
www.themarinaatroweswharf.com

Boater's Resources

Russo Marine
24-R Ericsson Street
Boston, MA 02122
617-288-1000
www.russomarine.com

Activities, Clubs, Nonprofits, and Museums

The Boston Harbor Association
374 Congress Street, Suite 307
Boston, MA 02210
617-482-1722
www.tbha.org

Boston Harbor Island Alliance
349 Lincoln Street
Hingham, MA 02043
781-740-4290
www.fbhi.org

Hingham Yacht Club
211 Downer Avenue
Hingham, MA 02043
781-749-9717
www.hinghamyachtclub.com

Hull Lifesaving Museum
1117 Nantasket Avenue
Hull, MA 02045
781-925-5433
www.hulllifesavingmuseum.org

Hull Yacht Club
5 Fitzpatrick Way
Hull, MA 02045
781-925-9739
www.hullyc.org

Island Alliance
408 Atlantic Avenue, Suite 228
Boston, MA 02110-8671
617-223-8672
www.islandalliance.org

Mass Audubon Society
208 South Great Road
Lincoln, MA 01773
781-259-9500
www.massaudubon.org

Nantasket Beach Salt Water Club
3 Fitzpatrick Way
Hull, MA 02045
781-925-9801
www.nbswc.org

New England Aquarium
Central Wharf
Boston, MA 02110
617-973-5200 (Main Number)
617-973-5206 (Whale Watch)
www.neaq.org

Save the Harbor/Save the Bay
Boston Fish Pier
212 Northern Avenue, Suite 304 West
Boston, MA 02210
617-451-2860
www.savetheharbor.org

Thompson Island Outward Bound
P.O. Box 127
Boston, MA 02127
617-328-3900
www.thompsonisland.org

Management Agencies & Other Governmental Resources

Boston Harbor Islands Partnership
408 Atlantic Avenue, Suite 225
Boston, MA 02110
617-223-8666
www.nps.gov/boha

City of Boston Environmental Department
City Archaeologist
152 North Street, Basement
Boston, MA 02113
617-635-3850
www.cityofboston.gov/environment

Department of Conservation and Recreation
251 Causeway Street, Suite 600
Boston, MA 02114
617-626-1250
www.mass.gov/dcr

Massachusetts Board of Underwater
Archaeological Resources
251 Causeway Street, Suite 800
Boston, MA 02114
617-626-1200
www.mass.gov/czm/buar

Massachusetts Water Resources Authority
Charlestown Navy Yard
100 First Avenue
Boston, MA 02129
617-242-6000
www.mwra.com

National Marine Fisheries Service
www.nmfs.noaa.gov

United States Coast Guard
408 Atlantic Avenue, #5
Boston, MA 02110
617-223-8600
www.ucsg.mil

Acknowledgements

This book was a pleasure to write, not just because of the many glorious days spent on the harbor islands, but because of the people I met along the way. I can only hope that their passion for the islands comes across on these pages.

I want to particularly thank: Chris Barnett, Ellen Berkland, Ralph DeGregorio, Bill and Claire Hale, Bruce Jacobson, Ron Killian, Elaine Kornbau, Vivien Li, Victor Mastone, Arthur Pearson, Tom Powers, Jay Schmidt, Sally Snowman, David Weinstein, and John Werner. My sincere thanks to Suzanne Gall Marsh and the volunteers of the Friends of the Boston Harbor Islands who shared their limitless knowledge, pictures, and, most important, love of the islands.

Nicole DeLaria, special collections librarian at The Bostonian Society, was of great assistance in tracking down research sources. Librarians Mary Lydon and Rebecca Kenney and communications specialist Barbara Allen at the Massachusetts Water Resources Authority helped with research on Deer Island and the cleanup of Boston Harbor. Thanks also to the librarians and archivists at the Boston Public Library, the State Library of Massachusetts, the Massachusetts Historical Society, the Massachusetts State Archives, the National Archives and Records Administration (Northeast Region), the Hingham Public Library, and the Howard Gotlieb Archival Research Center at Boston University.

I'm immensely grateful to Nicole Vecchiotti. Her enthusiasm and humor were invaluable in guiding this narrative. (And her rowing skills were invaluable in guiding me around the harbor.)

I'd like to thank my friends, family, and parents for all of their love and support. Finally, my eternal love goes to my wife, Erin, who indulged my many days spent island-hopping. This book wouldn't have been possible without her endless encouragement and inspiration.

In addition to those already mentioned, Union Park Press would also like to thank: Elizabeth Mock and Dale Freeman at the Archives and Special Collections Department of the Healey Library, University of Massachusetts Boston, Raj Sharma, Chuck Zonderman, Cherie Dube, Nelson Pidgeon, Patricia King Powers, Sherman "Pat" Morss, Jr., Julie Saunders, Elizabeth Lawrence, Jane & Mark Hirsh, Jay Hirsh, and Marah Hardt for her assistance in researching the natural history of the harbor islands. Last but not least, Amelia, Ethan, and Mark Vecchiotti—just because.